INSPIRING CONFIDENCE IN PROGRESS

• • •

INSPIRING CONFIDENCE IN PROGRESS

The History of O. R. Colan Associates

CATHERINE COLAN MUTH

Cover design by Richard G. Hypes

ISBN-13: 9780692790359
ISBN-10: 0692790357

DEDICATION

This book is dedicated to two people I loved and respected:

My father, Owen Richard Colan, who had the vision and entrepreneurial spirit to create a company that set new standards in the right of way industry; and

My grandmother, Lucille Colan, who helped make this book possible by lovingly collecting newspaper clippings about her son over the years.

They taught me that girls can do anything.

CREDITS

I want to acknowledge the guidance and assistance provided by Holly Strawbridge who interviewed all of the employees quoted in the book. Holly attempted to be my ghost writer but I kept interfering with her efforts to the point where the book became mine. Sorry, Holly! This book would have remained an unrealized dream without her support and direction.

My sincere thanks to Dick Moeller for the historical information in Chapters 1-3. Dick has been my mentor since joining ORC in 2002 after retiring from the Federal Highway Administration in Washington, D. C. as Program Manager of the Office of Real Estate Services. He often reviews my writing and has saved me from embarrassment on more than one occasion by catching errors before they were published.

A special thank you to Gary Scott, the honorary Historian of O. R. Colan Associates for being the keeper of so many documents and pictures from our past. He saw value where I saw clutter.

Many thanks to Tom Foster, my Vistage Chair of 20 years, who provided major edits and even recommended that I take it to the next level with more of a story line. Thank you, Tom. I will consider that in the next edition.

I would also like to express my appreciation for the employees who have played an important role in the success of our family business over the years. The stories many shared for this book are first-hand accounts of their journeys with my father and, later, with me in building our company.

The intended audience for this book is the employees of O. R. Colan Associates, LLC and our affiliate ORC Utility & Infrastructure Land Services, LLC. Our hope is that this book will give you a greater understanding of the history of our company and the legacy of our founder, Owen Richard Colan, J.D. While a broader audience is not expected, there may be people interested in the history of the Uniform Act and its impact on how the public is treated when eminent domain is used to acquire land for public infrastructure projects using federal funding.

OUR VISION STATEMENT: *INSPIRING CONFIDENCE IN PROGRESS*

If you were to ask 100 people what they think about eminent domain, their answers would be resoundingly negative. Few people like change. This is doubly true when their home or business lies in the path of progress. Based on the media's philosophy that "if it bleeds, it leads," the stories about people displaced for public projects are generally sad. Although most people become upset when they are told they must make way for progress, we receive many letters from property owners and occupants thanking us for the way we assisted them through the process with compassion and understanding. These letters are evidence that we are inspiring confidence in progress.

We believe that building the infrastructure of our country is an important endeavor, and we are proud to be part of this process. Our country's infrastructure is critical to public safety, well-being and progress. Each new highway, airport runway, school, water line, sewer project and transmission line signifies economic growth.

In the 1950s, President Dwight D. Eisenhower envisioned building an interstate highway system to enhance our national defense. My father, Owen Richard Colan, started our company in 1969 to help make this vital transportation system a reality.

Today, a new interstate transportation system is being created for moving energy. It requires rebuilding and expanding our electrical grid, as well as the transportation of oil and gas through the nation's network of pipelines. We formed ORC Utility and Infrastructure Land Services, LLC, in 2010 to help meet the growing needs of this sector.

Our Mission Statement says we strive to reduce stress on those who are required to sell their property or relocate for public works projects. We understand how stressful the moving process can be, even when a family or business chooses to move. The 5th Amendment to the U.S. Constitution[1] was enacted to ensure just compensation when private property is acquired for public use. The Uniform Relocation Assistance and Real Property Acquisition Act of 1970, as amended ("Uniform Act") protects both the real and personal property rights of people impacted by public works projects that use federal funding.

Eminent domain can be part of this process, but our goal is to reach a negotiated settlement, and our settlement rate is usually more than 90%[2]. Of course, the media only wants stories about the properties that are acquired through eminent domain. Without eminent domain our highways would be a tangled maze around property owners who refuse to sell.

Our agents respect the private property rights of those who are impacted by public works projects and ensure their rights are protected throughout the process. When a family or business is relocated, we see that those involved receive all the benefits to which they are entitled under both the federal law (the Uniform Act) and state law. Our expertise in the Uniform Act and in applicable state laws allows relocated property owners, tenants and businesses to move confidently through this stressful process.

---

1 The 5th Amendment to the U.S. Constitution states "No person shall be held to answer for a capital or otherwise infamous crime unless on a presentment or indictment of a grand jury, except in cases arising in the land or naval forces, or in the militia, when in actual service in time of war or public danger; nor shall any person be subject for the same offense to be twice put in jeopardy of life or limb; nor shall be compelled in any criminal case to be a witness against himself, **nor be deprived of** life, liberty, or **property without due process of law; nor shall private property be taken for public use without just compensation."**

2 The more time that is allowed in a project schedule for negotiations, the higher the negotiated settlement rate. The opposite is also true.

By honoring our company's values—

Respect, Knowledge, Integrity
Stewardship, Social Responsibility
Problem Solving, Initiative and Adaptability

We inspire our clients and the public to believe and trust in progress. That is the essence of our Vision Statement: ***inspiring confidence in progress.***

Karen S. Ammar   Catherine Colan Muth
Chairman   Chief Executive Officer

O.R. Colan Associates, LLC / ORC Training
ORC Utility & Infrastructure Land Services, LLC

TABLE OF CONTENTS

PREFACE

O. R. Colan Associates (ORC) is named for my father, Owen Richard Colan, JD, who was known as Dick and fondly called "Mr. C." by those who had the privilege of working with him. Our company's success was built on his vision.

He founded ORC to provide right-of-way services for state agencies involved in building the country's Interstate Highway System. His approach to right of way acquisition fundamentally changed the business model for how real estate is acquired for public projects. His vision of using right of way consultants for the land acquisition phase of interstate highway construction is today the norm nationwide for public works projects.

My father liked to say, "When it looks like a lost deal, figure out how to make it happen."

After graduating from Georgetown Law School in 1947, his first job was to buy land for the new West Virginia Turnpike. This was where he discovered his career in public sector real estate, also known as the right of way industry. Our story begins with the following illustration of how his persistence paid off. In this March 26, 1955, *Saturday Evening Post* article, author Richard Thruelsen explained how my father worked long into the night using gentle persuasion to help a reluctant landowner make a difficult decision:

> *Acquiring the $7,000,000 worth of real estate necessary to provide a 250-foot-plus right of way for the new (WV) turnpike was less of a problem*

than might be expected, because much of the new road runs through wilderness and rural areas. Dick Colan, the Turnpike Commission's chief right of way agent, and his agile staff climbed up and down the hills for two years before they had the eighty-eight mile strip bought and paid for. The smallest purchase made by Colan's men was a patch of ground covering fourteen square feet, and the largest was five miles of the right of way owned by a coal company.

"We had very little trouble," reports Colan. "Nobody shot at us and we didn't stumble over any stills. Before we'd finished we found we bought, in addition to the land, eight hundred and eighty houses, twelve churches, six schools and two small coal mines blocked off by the turnpike. We also bought five farms that had nothing to do with the highway, but they were situated far up a mountain draw that was completely blocked by the turnpike. Building another access road to them was impractical, so we just bought out the owners and let the farms go. We relocated eleven cemeteries and part of one gasoline refinery and, altogether, spend two million dollars relocating utility lines that crossed the right of way. Our two guiding rules were never to argue and always to call on farmers after the chores are done."

Following this principle, Colan called one rural widow shortly after dinner one night.

The aging lady listened intently to Colan's explanation of the turnpike project and to the commission's offer for her property, but seemed reluctant to make a decision, so Colan went through his explanation and his sales talk once again. Still the widow remained undecided.

"About nine o'clock," recalls Colan, "the lady's forty-year-old son came in and silently folded himself into a rocking chair. So I went through my pitch once again. When the widow appealed to her son for an opinion, all he offered was, "I ain't saying, mom." So we talked some more, but all we could get out of the son was that, "I ain't saying, mom." Finally, about midnight, I realized I was getting nowhere, so I left. The son saw me to the door and came out onto the porch with me. Suddenly I had an idea. "Look," I said to the son, "if you had said something in there, what would you have said?" "Why, Mr. Colan,' he says, "I would have said, "Sell it, Mom."

Colan had the widow's signature on the option five minutes later.

PART I
MY FATHER'S STORY
1947 - 1989

Chapter 1

● ● ●

HISTORY OF THE INTERSTATE HIGHWAY SYSTEM

THE VISION FOR AN INTERSTATE HIGHWAY SYSTEM

In 1919, a young lieutenant colonel in the U.S. Army named Dwight D. Eisenhower was in a convoy of military vehicles that traversed the country from Washington, DC, to San Francisco. The drive was undertaken to gain an understanding of the difficulties involved in moving large numbers of military troops and vehicles around the nation. The nation had no cohesive road system connecting the states, so the convoy only averaged 5 mph. Eisenhower found this pace to be frustrating and depressing, but he would not be in a position to effect changes for another 35 years.[3]

By the late 1930s, the pressure for constructing a transcontinental highway system was getting stronger. It reached the White House, where President Franklin D. Roosevelt repeatedly expressed interest in constructing a network of toll highways in order to provide more jobs for people who were out of work during the depression.

President Roosevelt thought three east-west and three north-south routes would be sufficient. Congress decided to explore the concept, and in 1938, directed the chief of the Bureau of Public Roads[4] to study the feasibility of a

---

3 For more information see "Ike's Interstates at 50" by David A. Pfeiffer.

4 The Bureau of Public Roads was renamed the Federal Highway Administration (FHWA) on October 15, 1966.

six-route toll network. The resulting report, *Toll Roads and Free Roads*, was based on planning surveys and analyses. But World War II intervened, and no immediate action was taken. It wasn't until Eisenhower was elected president that the interstate highway system became a reality.

THE FEDERAL-AID HIGHWAY ACT OF 1954

Car and truck traffic boomed in the post-war years, and the need for better roads and a strong interstate highway system became clear. President Eisenhower remembered the difficulties of his 1919 trip, driving across the country on local roads. In 1954, he told the nation that an interstate highway system was important to national security. Congress quickly enacted the Federal-Aid Highway Act of 1954, which allocated $175 million in federal funds to the project. These moneys would be matched 60-40 by the states using a complicated formula based on population, road distance and land area.

At the time, the acquisition of property for highways and public works projects was handled by state right of way employees. These state agents had varying backgrounds and capabilities, but most came from the real estate brokerage and property management fields. The process was neither fair nor uniform, and agents did not always treat property owners kindly or fairly.

Most often, land acquisition for a public project was accomplished in two steps: First, the property was appraised, then an offer was made. Laws varied from state to state. In most states, property owners were not compensated for moving or reimbursed for relocation expenses.

"A property owner might have received a letter stating: 'Here is the offer, take it or leave it,'" explained Dick Moeller, who came to work for ORC in 2002 after retiring from 30 years of service with the Federal Highway Administration (FHWA). "Alternatively, you might have been summoned to the acquiring agency's office or to an attorney in their employ and advised of the need to acquire property from you."

"You might have only received a verbal offer of how much they would pay you," continues Moeller. "The agency would often use a process generally referred to as 'horse trading,' which involved a series of offers and counteroffers between the parties. If no agreement was reached by the end of this process—whether it was a take-it-or-leave-it offer or a negotiation—a condemnation suit was filed.

"This process tended to favor property owners who were affluent, knowledgeable about the process or able afford legal counsel," says Moeller. "The elderly, women and those who were uninformed about their rights under applicable law were often taken advantage of. Practices were often coercive, such as lowballing offers well below the estimated value of the property or threatening the owner with condemnation or eviction."

Eisenhower's Interstate Highway System called for 43,000 miles of a four-lane, access-controlled highway, which required the purchase of thousands of land parcels. Not surprisingly, the land acquisition process took years to accomplish. Questionable practices came to the attention of the Bureau of Public Roads and the U.S. Congress as people complained of mistreatment by right-of-way agents. Responding to this public outcry, the U.S. Bureau of Public Roads developed policies and procedures regarding land acquisitions using federal funds. Unfortunately, its agency policies and procedures had non-regulatory[5] status at the time, state participation was often difficult to achieve, and some states failed to fully adopt the policies advocated by the Bureau of Public Roads.

Simultaneously, the U.S. Bureau of Public Roads increased their staff of real estate appraisal and acquisition experts by hiring recent college graduates and training them appropriately. Dick Moeller was in the first right-of-way training class, held in 1963.

In the mid-to-late 1960s, various state and federal agencies worked on a wide variety of projects aimed at expanding and improving the nation's infrastructure. These included projects for urban renewal, flood control, electric power generation, airport expansions, highways and mass transit. All of these

---

5 Policies and procedures do not in themselves have the force of law. A federal law is passed by Congress and signed by the President, while a state law is passed by the state legislature and signed by the Governor. The appropriate agency then prepares regulations explaining how the law is to be implemented, and these rules or regulations are adopted through a formal rule-making process. An agency which must conform to a law and implementing regulations is responsible for writing policies and procedures describing how it will operate a compliant program. The policies and procedures developed by the Bureau of Public Roads were not a formal regulation that had the force and effect of law, but were recommended procedures to be followed to qualify for Federal Funding reimbursement.

public works projects required extensive real estate acquisition and created a market need for right of way consultants like ORC.

THE NATIONAL ENVIRONMENTAL PROTECTION ACT OF 1969 (NEPA)

The environmental impact of these large, federally funded projects throughout the nation became a concern and resulted in the passing of the Federal National Environmental Protection Act of 1969 (NEPA). This act focused on the social and economic impacts of these projects, as well as their environmental impact.

NEPA created new challenges for right-of-way professionals. In the process of appraising property and offering fair compensation, agents had to consider environmental impact and social justice issues. An example of a social justice issue was insufficient replacement housing. In those cases, NEPA required that additional housing be built. In other cases, where wetland mitigation was needed, NEPA required the agency to acquire additional land to mitigate wetland and habitat destruction.

After NEPA passed, multiple lawsuits were filed, alleging that many public agencies had not complied with its requirements. As a result, courts often blocked agencies from moving forward on projects.

THE UNIFORM RELOCATION AND REAL PROPERTIES ACQUISITION POLICIES ACT ("UNIFORM ACT") OF 1970

Accomplishing right-of-way acquisition became increasingly complex. Growing furor prompted Congress to hold investigations and hearings over the treatment of property owners, individuals, businesses and farms whose properties were needed for public projects. The result was passage of the Uniform Relocation and Real Properties Acquisition Policies Act ("Uniform Act") of 1970. Compliance was no longer optional. Any public agency receiving federal funds for any phase of a project was required to follow the procedures set forth by the Uniform Act.

This important legislation became the core of services offered by ORC.

Chapter 2

THE RIGHT MAN FOR RIGHT OF WAY

My father was proud to participate in building the nation's infrastructure and recognized its importance. The infrastructure projects he worked on, and that ORC works on today, are the foundation of progress in our country and our communities.

Even before Eisenhower set about linking the states, West Virginia politicians began discussing the need for a highway system that would link their state to Ohio, Virginia and North Carolina. With approval of the state legislature, West Virginia Governor Okey Patteson established a Turnpike Commission in 1947 and instituted a traffic survey. The engineers concluded that a two-lane turnpike connecting Charleston with Princeton would pay for itself, with 70 percent of the revenue in 1955 coming from truck traffic.

Raised in South Charleston, WV, my father attended public schools there and continued his education at Bethany College before receiving a Bachelor of Arts degree from West Virginia University. He then served in the Naval Air Corps during World War II. After the war he entered Georgetown University Law School and graduated with a law degree in 1947. He was looking for a job after graduation and was hired as Assistant to the State Right of Way Engineer and Special Assistant Attorney General for the State Road Commission of West Virginia. In 1952, he was made Chief Right of Way Agent for the West Virginia Turnpike Commission.

In this position, my father bought 88 miles of property for the two-lane turnpike through West Virginia. (It later became a section of I-77 through the southern part of the state).

Much of the land in West Virginia needed for turnpike construction was rural or undeveloped, and most parcels were purchased in just two years. Although the state had only enough funds to build a two-lane highway, they acquired enough land to expand the turnpike to four lanes using federal funds. The initial two-lane highway was completed in 1952 but the additional lanes needed to meet interstate standards were not completed until 1986.[6]

Some residents felt a four-lane version of the highway should be built earlier than planned. In fact, just two weeks after construction began, the *Charleston Gazette* demanded that a four-lane highway be built. Construction came to a halt, but resumed shortly after a judge ruled against the newspaper, saying that the state was building a four-lane highway—albeit two lanes at a time.

The West Virginia Turnpike finally opened in 1955 at a cost of $1,500,000 per mile. The astronomical price tag (for that time) was in part due to the state's mountainous terrain, which required 76 bridges.

By late 1956 the state Turnpike Commission's right of-way department was no longer needed. On December 31, 1956, the department disbanded after its two remaining members—my father and his assistant, T. A. Knotts[7]— departed. My father left the post he had held for four years and entered the private practice of law in Charleston.

He sold his house to fund his start-up law practice, with my mother, Ruth, as his secretary. I was their only child. We moved in temporarily with my widowed grandmother, Lucille Colan.

---

6 *Dick Moeller was in WV as the FHWA ROW Officer in the early 1970s and recalls that the WV DOT was buying additional ROW for the WV Turnpike to bring it up to the Interstate Highway System standards. This may only have been required in some sections, but sufficient ROW had not been acquired originally for construction of four lanes for the entire 77 miles.*

Another interesting aspect of the upgrading of the WV Turnpike, was that it was the first time that Interstate Highway System funding was used to upgrade a toll road and allow the agency to still collect the tolls, which it is still doing today. It was through the political power of the WV Congressional delegation that this was accomplished. It created a precedent for a similar decision later to fund other toll road projects with federal money.

7 *T. A. "Tom" Knotts later became a high-level right of way manager at FHWA.*

My father always made time to spend with his family. A favorite weekend pastime was fishing, and one of our family traditions is to set a hook in your parent. I managed to hook my father's hand and, many years later, my son got a hook attached so firmly in the top of my head that had to be removed by a doctor. Fishing taught me patience, which is important to success in business, because you have to put your line in the water so many times before you land a job.[8]

After a year in law practice, my father tired of handling divorce cases—the core of his legal business—and accepted the position as Right of Way Officer for the Pennsylvania office of the U.S. Bureau of Public Roads. In late 1958, the family moved to Harrisburg, Pennsylvania, where we stayed for four years. During this time my father developed strong relationships with this federal agency (later called FHWA) that is designated under the Uniform Act as the lead agency for all federally funded projects involving land acquisition.

TAKING THE LEAD IN WEST VIRGINIA

In 1962, my father was invited back home to serve as Director of the newly created Right of Way Division of the State Road Commission of West Virginia. He served under State Road Commissioner Burl Sawyers, who called his appointment "part of an announced plan to reorganize the state's largest governmental department."[9]

The state was about to receive significant funding for interstate highway work. It is probable that my father's former employer, the Bureau of Public Roads, recognized that the state lacked the necessary competent people to handle the job and recommended hiring him to put the right of way acquisition program in order. The state knew it had to comply with new federal

---

8 *On the same day that my son, Kevin (around age 8) fulfilled his duty to hook his parent, he also got impatient that the fish were not biting. The lake had been stocked that day, and the fish were still dazed. He noticed several fish close to shore and just walked in and grabbed one, showing both problem solving skills and initiative at a very early age!*

9 *Charleston Gazette-Mail,* November 11, 1962

procedures or risk losing millions of dollars in federal funding for its highway construction.

I remember my father saying that he was invited to be Director of Right of Way for the state of West Virginia as part of a larger movement to "clean up government" in that state. Wally Barron had been elected governor in 1960 and quickly gained a reputation for corruption, which did not go unnoticed by the federal Bureau of Public Roads. The agency was reluctant to invest large sums of money in the West Virginia Interstate highway program under Governor Barron without someone who could be trusted as Director of Right of Way. Governor Barron later served a prison term for jury tampering.

Without delay, my father made the changes he felt were necessary to meet the needs of the state's expanding highway program and comply with federal regulations. The processes he established were some of the first of their kind and changed the way right of way would be conducted in the future.

His first change was to institute civil service status for right-of-way agents, appraisers, engineers and trainees. This was a paradigm shift, as typically such positions in state government were filled through patronage. Historically, eligibility depended not on qualifications or ability to do the job, but on political connections. Relying on unqualified persons in patronage positions to conduct important negotiations with and provide services to property owners often caused problems.

He recruited qualified personnel for appraisal and engineering and added trained negotiators to assist in the district offices. In direct contrast to the common practice of using real estate agents without right of way experience, he hired bright young college graduates and trained them in the methods of acquiring right of way in compliance with state and federal requirements.[10] Public agencies would later follow his lead. This innovative approach forever changed the public's perception of land acquisition agents.

In March 1963, my father moved the division offices to facilities that were better suited for expanded operations and activities. Floor space was tripled, permitting new engineering equipment to be installed, along with the

---

10 ORC continues this practice today in our Junior Agent program.

drafting tables and printing machines necessary to develop right of way, utility adjustment plans and legal descriptions.

He established a control room in which information on the status of every parcel and utility adjustment item for each project was visible from a central point in the room. This control room put current information at the fingertips of everyone involved in every project in an era before computers. He called this room "the nerve center for right of way acquisition."

To improve communication with the public, he wrote a brochure that answered questions his agents commonly encountered in the process of negotiating for property. The agents personally delivered the brochure to affected property owners during their first contact. Today, such brochures are typically used by all land acquisition agencies when federal funding is involved and are generally specific to the phase of the project: appraisal, acquisition, relocation assistance or property management.

My father also initiated a research section. Its first task was to conduct a severance damage study along I-64 from Charleston to Huntington. Considerable data was gathered and compiled into individual case studies for publication and distribution. This initiative was the forerunner of similar such land economic studies undertaken later by other states. These studies proved very helpful to appraisers analyzing impacts that caused a decrease or increase in the value of the remaining property after partial acquisition of right of way for a highway project. The "severance damage" studies documented market conditions and analyzed the subsequent sale of remainder properties, noting how they had or had not been impacted by the partial acquisition.

Appraisers used the empirical data from these studies to prepare accurate, substantiated value estimates in their appraisal reports. Severance damage studies also provided persuasive evidence in litigation during trials or settlement proceedings with affected property owners.

He also added a relocation advisory assistance section to the department to aid the relocation of families and businesses displaced by highway construction. This section handled reimbursements for moving costs. Such reimbursements were authorized under legislation enacted by the 1963 session of the

West Virginia legislature, following federal authorization of such payments to displaced residents.

TRAINING AND OPERATING PROCEDURES

Two bold initiatives that distinguished this pioneering approach to right of way involved the development of uniform operating procedures and the training of staff to implement these procedures effectively.

First, he prepared an operations and procedures manual, which was distributed to all right of way personnel. The manual was based on the American Association of State Highway Officials (AASHO)[11] publication called *Acquisition for Right of Way*. The manual detailed the practice and procedures of a right of way division and encompassed organization, administration, engineering, appraisals, negotiation, condemnation, property management, utilities, titles, deeds, records, reports and relocation advisory assistance. Standard definitions, forms and pertinent federal aid regulations were also included.

Second, he instituted a program of continuing education to create a pipeline of qualified personnel. He appointed a training officer with the education and experience to present an efficient, comprehensive study course. Leading professionals in various fields of the State Road Commission, recognized instructors from private enterprise, professional educators and high-level personnel from the Washington headquarters and regional offices of the U.S. Bureau of Public Roads were selected as instructors. The course was divided into four instructional units: legal principles, engineering principles, appraisal principles and negotiation principles. All right of way agents, appraisers and trainees were required to complete the course.

To support these educational efforts, my father established a library and stocked it with all recognized publications pertaining to right of way acquisition, negotiation skills, appraisal and utility relocation.

---

11 The American Association of State Highway Officials (AASHO) was renamed The American Association of State Highway and Transportation Officials (AASHTO) on November 13, 1973.

CHALLENGES OF RIGHT OF WAY ACQUISITION IN WEST VIRGINIA

During my father's tenure in West Virginia, he oversaw right of way acquisition and relocation assistance for sections of Interstates 64, 77 and 79 passing through West Virginia. Approximately 1,400 families in Kanawha County were displaced by the construction of these roads. He put in place policies that ensured everyone was treated fairly.

At the time, West Virginia was one of 18 states that paid moving costs up to $200 for displaced families and up to $3,000 for displaced businesses. The passage of the Federal Aid Highway Act of 1968 raised those amounts. On September 23, 1968, *The Charleston Daily Mail* reported that, "… effective last August 23, persons whose homes are taken for road construction may receive up to $5,000 above the fair market value of their houses, and payment up to $1,500 is authorized to a displaced tenant to rent new quarters or apply the money as down payment on the purchase of a home." These changes indicated a trend toward recognizing the impact of building the Interstate Highway System on homeowners and businesses. This legislation affected only highway acquisition programs, but was a precursor to passage of the Uniform Act in 1970 that required compliance by all Federal agencies.

Although the vast majority of relocations were routine, some were memorable. A renter with 109 parakeets, 11 cats and a dog was one of many atypical situations that ORC agents encountered. "How do you relocate them when they're sitting in the middle of a future interstate highway? You remain patient and you persevere," said my father in a 1968 *Charleston Daily Mail* article.

In this particular situation, the ORC agent took the renter to view prospective places every week, but she declined every option. Nearly one year passed before her minister and friends convinced her to select a new residence. When she finally moved, she found her new home to be entirely satisfactory.

Eight engineering firms and 33 contractors worked around the clock on the construction of the Interstate highway system through West Virginia. The rocky, uneven, mountainous terrain proved challenging and required 76 bridges and tunnels that had to be blasted through solid rock. Landslides and hidden water sources caused headaches and delays.

In addition to the physical challenges, construction was slowed when a group known as the Triangle Area Improvement Council raised objections to the way displaced residents in a predominantly minority neighborhood known as the Triangle Area adjacent to the central business district of Charleston, WV, were supposedly being treated. The protesters invoked NEPA, alleging adverse sociological impact to the neighborhood and lack of fair housing for displaced residents.

The ability to build the interstate as designed was critical, since geography limited any alternatives. The Triangle Area was located in a relatively narrow valley bordered on both sides by mountainous terrain. Avoiding this area would have interrupted the continuity of the interstate highway system through the Mid-Atlantic States since this was to be the intersection of Interstates 64, 77 and 79.

The protests led to hearings. My father was the first defense witness called to the stand. He testified that his team of 10 encountered no serious problems in the relocation process. Indeed, they did everything possible to ensure that residents of the area obtained proper housing. The agents personally contacted the residents, advised them of available housing options, took them to see these options and inspected the potential properties to make sure they met FHWA criteria for decent, safe and sanitary housing.

Moreover, no one was forced to move. If a homeowner or renter was unable to relocate after title to the property was acquired, the occupants were permitted to continue residing under the same terms that existed with the previous owner until an acceptable resolution could be reached.

Many challenging relocation cases were presented by this project. One was the relocation of an eligible displacee[12] who resided in a 1956 De Soto automobile. A brothel was also displaced, creating some interesting relocation assistance challenges. Additionally, one or more of the displaced residents were in jail.

Ultimately, the state was allowed to proceed. My father acquired the necessary property and successfully relocated all owners and tenants under the watchful eyes of the FHWA and the U.S. Department of Transportation's Office of Civil Rights, which was sued along with the state of West Virginia.

---

12 A "displacee" is a person or a business that is displaced by a public project.

It was the beginning of a major change in how right of way acquisition was conducted.

COLAN'S OPINION INFLUENCES CONGRESS

My father's leadership was acknowledged when he was appointed to leadership positions in the American Association of State Highway Officials (AASHO) and the American Right of Way Association.[1]

As Chairman of the AASHO Right of Way Committee, he was able to influence the development of federal requirements and regulations by testifying before Congressional lawmakers. In his first hearing, he spoke to a proposed federal regulation that would provide for at least two public hearings on any highway project utilizing federal funds. The West Virginia State Road Commission and agencies of other states objected to portions of these regulations, including one that would apparently enable any individual to file repeated objections, delaying highway projects. But my father's opinion was highly respected, and lawmakers moved to allow the public multiple hearings.

Challenges to the way right of way was being acquired by the states for the Interstate Highway System were not limited to the acquisition processes in West Virginia. In the February 4, 1962 edition of Parade magazine, widely syndicated investigative reporter Jack Anderson wrote about "The Great Highway Robbery." He quoted Representative John A. Blatnik (D-MN), head of the Special Subcommittee on the Federal-Aid Highway Program that was investigating the allegations of corruption in right of way acquisition, as saying "Corruption permeates the highway program and stigmatizes the whole road-building industry."[2] The Blatnik hearings led to continued attention to the failure of the program to provide fair treatment to property owners impacted by the Interstate Highway Program.

---

[1] Chairman, Highway Research Board Committee on Land Acquisition, 1966-1969; Chairman, National Highway Committee of the American Right of Way Association, 1967-1969; Chairman, AASHO Right of Way Subcommittee on Administration and Manpower Utilization, 1963-1967; Chairman, AASHO Right of Way Committee, 1968–1969

[2] Quoted from *The Greatest Decade 1956 – 1966*, FHWA publication commemorating the 50th anniversary of the Eisenhower Interstate Highway System.

As a result of the findings of the Blatnik Committee, the Bureau of Public Roads began to design a new piece of legislation that would protect the 5th and 14th Amendments to the U. S. Constitution guaranteeing "just compensation" and "due process." The ultimate result was the Uniform Relocation and Real Property Acquisition Policies Act of 1970 ("Uniform Act"), which transformed the way the public was treated when land was needed for any federally funded public project.

Chapter 3

● ● ●

COLAN SETS NEW STANDARDS IN THE INDUSTRY

n the late 1960s, Congress realized the nation needed a fair and equitable way of treating people forced to relinquish their property for a public project. They began to discuss the creation of a law that would establish minimum standards for federally funded programs and projects requiring the acquisition of property or resulting in the displacement of persons from their homes, businesses or farms. The law they created is known as the Uniform Relocation and Real Property Acquisition Policies Act of 1970 ("Uniform Act").[13]

---

13 Agencies using federal funds for any part of a project are required to follow Uniform Act regulations, found at 49 CFR Part 24. The law provides for relocation assistance to lessen the emotional and financial impact of displacement. It ensures that no one is displaced from their home unless decent, safe and sanitary replacement housing is available within their financial means. This improves the housing conditions of displaced persons living in substandard housing. The act requires that every effort be made to accomplish acquisition by agreement and without coercion.

Anyone displaced by a federal-aid project must be given full relocation benefits, including:

* Advisory assistance
* Interest differential between their existing mortgage and a new mortgage for residential occupants
* Cost differential between the appraised value of their home and the cost of a comparable replacement home
* Reimbursement of reasonable costs associated with moving, including the costs to move home furnishings, disconnect and reconnect utilities and other incidental expenses.

Businesses are entitled to receive reimbursement for the cost of moving to a new location, including the cost to disconnect and reconnect heavy equipment and to move inventory. The moving costs sometimes amount to more than the cost of the property that is being acquired.

In 1969, seeing the Uniform Act on the horizon, my father realized the potential for private right of way consultants. He felt consultants would be particularly useful for highway departments, which were often overstaffed or understaffed between acquisition projects. He was confident a private firm could handle these jobs more efficiently by hiring qualified personnel and moving them from state to state as new projects arose, thus affording better management of staffing for state right or way agencies. He believed that this approach would allow state agencies to lower their personnel costs by retaining only those employees needed to handle day-to-day operations. So in late November 1969, he resigned as Right of Way Director for the West Virginia State Road Commission and formed O. R. Colan Associates, Inc., of Florida.

Florida was one of the first states to hire outside consultants for highway-related right of way acquisition services. As soon as the Uniform Act became law, the Florida DOT's right of way acquisition program found itself in trouble. The state had started the construction of Interstate 95 (I-95) in Miami, with 90 percent of funding provided by the federal government. But the state's appraisal and appraisal review processes failed to comply with the Uniform Act, and the FHWA announced it would withhold $50 million in federal funding until mistakes were corrected. The state was issued a Federal Agency Ineligibility Notice (FAIN) by FHWA.

Construction of I-95 in Broward County came to a halt due to failure of the appraisal process to comply with FHWA requirements. With completion of the project in jeopardy, the state hired O. R. Colan Associates of Florida, Inc. (ORC) to train new appraisers and proceed with acquiring the properties needed to build the remaining 11 miles of interstate in Broward and Palm Beach counties. ORC was also asked to retrospectively re-document $50 million in right of way reimbursement claims that had not been substantiated, so the state could recover expenditures that had not been reimbursed by the FHWA.

MR. COLAN: A GIFTED TEACHER

When Florida hired ORC to complete right of way acquisition for I-95, an insufficient number of qualified appraisers were available to do the work. As the first step in bringing the project into compliance, my father arranged to train a class of appraisers for the Florida DOT.

He set up a classroom in a warehouse that was condemned and acquired for right of way. Bob Pratt, who worked for him as the primary appraisal instructor at the West Virginia DOT, was hired to teach most of the courses. My father taught condemnation law and eminent domain law. Bob Gallion, a local appraiser, was retained and served as a hands-on training consultant.

"You knew you were talking to someone who knew the game, not just a manager without technical expertise," said Gallion about my father.

He remembers how my father taught agents how to value partial takings. "You value the property as a whole, then you value the part that will be taken. Finally, you value what's left. If there's a difference between the total and what's left, less the part taken, you have damages," he explains.

My father used clever examples to illustrate his points. Sometimes, he'd call a student in front of the class and say, "That's a beautiful tie. What do you think it's worth, class?" Then he'd cut off the back of the tie. "Now what's it worth? It still has a front part," he'd say. Then he'd clip off the front and ask, "Now what's it worth?"

Other times, he'd buy a blouse for a woman in the class. He'd cut off one sleeve and say, "Now what's it worth? You can always alter it and make the other sleeve shorter."

Ed Wilson, another local appraiser, was a member of this appraisal class. He remembers these examples clearly. "They were very funny and had good shock value. More importantly, they were effective in helping us remember the points he made," he says.

Another instruction technique my father used when he wanted to underscore the need for acute observation when inspecting properties was to walk in with several bricks and ask the class, "What do you think I have here?" The answer was always, "You have some bricks." Picking up a brick, he'd say, "You sure about that?" Then he'd throw it at a student. It was Styrofoam.

"He was teaching that things aren't always what they appear," says Wilson.

The lessons stuck, because they were interesting. "We learned a lot of different things. I still remember the difference between clapboard, lapboard and drop siding—which has no application in South Florida whatsoever," Wilson remembers with a laugh.

The first class of 24 students spent six months in classwork and 18 months in the field. When they finished, they were well prepared to handle appraisal and acquisition. "We were just out of college, and in six months we were doing more complicated work than people who had been at the DOT for 10 years," says Wilson.

After graduation, the agents stayed with the Florida DOT for several years, until all parcels of I-95 in Broward and Palm Beach were acquired, and the condemnation process was complete.

ORC: A NEW KIND OF COMPANY

My father's success in reinstating the $50 million in federal funds to the Florida highway program gave him a solid reputation as a technical expert who could get also the job done. His company was off to a good start.

Establishing the first private right of way consulting company specializing in right of way services for the public sector gave him the opportunity to instill his values and way of doing business from the start. He set out to create a company that would be defined by the values that were later formally defined as

* Respect
* Knowledge
* Integrity
* Stewardship
* Social Responsibility
* Initiative
* Adaptability
* Problem Solving

To carry out his mission, he hired agents who were smart, compassionate and willing to learn.

My father understood that a right of way agent's duties had changed. "Once he (the right of way agent) was only an engineer, but now he must be a qualified appraiser, real estate agent, attorney, family counselor, psychologist and public relations man, as well as an engineer," he said in a magazine article (*FC&E*, August, 1970). "The ROW agent is the only man the public ever sees, and he must be the best we have."

He established ORC as an employee-based company, rather than using 1099 employees. It was his way of ensuring he always had the personnel necessary to do a job, and that his agents met his high standards. He could hire men and women with potential, train them to be agents, give them experience and monitor their performance over time. He also took advantage of using part time employees from the West Virginia Highway Department who worked evenings and weekends at ORC. Gary Scott is one of those employees who has worked in this capacity for more than 40 years.

In acquisition agents, my father looked for specific personal characteristics:

* Extroverted personality
* Good people skills
* Sales skills
* Analytical skills
* Attention to detail
* Ability to keep excellent records.

For appraisals—a job one agent called "part art, part science and part research"—he looked for someone willing to learn the laws, rules and regulations pertaining to the appraisal of real property and possessing the analytical skills to apply these conditions to different situations.

"You had to be able to take the heat and have empathy," says Ted Pluta, who was hired in 1985. "He gave new hires a six-month probation period to see how they did. He expected you to know your business."

My father had a knack for hiring good people who were capable of doing their jobs.

Daryl Knobbe was hired in 1984 as an office manager. He liked ORC so much that he became a trainee agent and now serves as one of ORC's Regional Vice Presidents and a member of the Leadership Team. "We expect our people to be professionals, so we treat them that way. They have to take ownership of what they are doing. There is no time clock. There is simply an expectation that we will get things done," he says.

My father built employee loyalty by offering generous salaries and good benefits (for the 1970s).

Ed Wilson was making $7,500 at the DOT when my father hired him in 1974. They agreed on a salary of $15,000, but Wilson found his monthly $1,500 paychecks actually added up to $18,000—which was considered a pretty good salary in 1974.

A former employee of the DOT, Bob Gallion was working as an appraiser at a mortgage company for $5,000 a year when my father offered him a job for $12,000. "I remember thinking, 'Wow! He could have hired me for a whole lot less.' But I guess he figured that's what the job was worth," says Gallion.

My father sought to create a quality business that he could control. Size was not his priority. While he was alive, ORC never had more than 30 to 50 full-time and 10 to 20 part-time employees.

"I don't think he was monetarily motivated. He cared more about having his company as his family than maximizing profits," says Wilson. "He never thought about how much he could charge a client. He just wanted to do the job and get a reasonable return."

Dick Colan was a tough boss, but a fair one. He knew his business inside and out and exuded an air of authority. "He had a reputation for being somewhat difficult to deal with, but his employees respected him. Nine out of 10 times, he was right," says Knobbe.

Offices were often housed in free space wrangled from clients. These spaces could be less than ideal. ORC's first office in Tampa had no air conditioning or restroom. But in a small space surrounded by hand-picked employees, my father was a happy man.

"He was devoted to his employees," says Wilson.

RIGHT OF WAY AS A SERVICE

Unlike some of his predecessors with state highway departments, who gave right of way a bad name, my father felt it was a privilege to serve his clients and the public, and he insisted that both be treated fairly.

His service in the Navy during World War II influenced how he conducted business. He considered his consulting work to be service to the public and felt honored to be part of the effort to build our nation's infrastructure.

His philosophy was to treat everyone equally, whether they were a leader in the community or living in poverty. Moreover, he strongly advocated that the client is always right.

Bob Gallion remembers my father saying, "Clients don't want to hear how smart you are; they want to hear how smart they are. When something goes wrong, the consultant must take the blame."

"He used to say there were three important things to remember: First, the client is always right. Second, the client is always right. Third, the client is always right," Gallion recounts.

A master of human psychology, Colan taught his agents to bring issues to a client's attention in an indirect way. "He taught us to say, 'Some people do it this way or that way' instead of suggesting that their system was inferior. It was really good advice, and it's applicable to a lot of situations," says Gallion.

OTHER VENTURES

Like many entrepreneurs, my father had many ideas that took him in various directions. Some did not work out as expected.

Around the same time he formed O. R. Colan Associates, Inc. of Florida, he partnered with an engineer named Don Rude to form a company called Colan-Rude and Associates. They figured this partnership would allow Don Rude to design roads and Colan to purchase the right of way. But the only projects they won were water projects with no need for right of way. In short order, they decided to dissolve the partnership and remain friends.

He also partnered with an African-American couple to form a disadvantaged business enterprise (DBE) in West Virginia they called Lewis-Colan, Ltd.

As a small minority owned firm, they were able to qualify as a Disadvantaged Business Enterprise (DBE) which gave the company an advantage when bidding on federally funded projects. The company was dissolved in November 2008, but had been inactive for more than a decade.

Because local companies believed they had an advantage when seeking work with a state highway department, he formed Tennessee Right of Way Associates in 1981 to seek work in the state of Tennessee. The company became inactive and was closed in 1992.

In 1971, he formed O. R. Colan Associates, Inc. of West Virginia, which became the company that outlasted all of his other business ventures.

Chapter 4

● ● ●

THE GROWTH YEARS

My father's concept of using consultants for the right of way phase of high-way projects began to take hold. His first highway project was for I-95 in Broward and Palm Beach Counties in Florida in 1970. This was followed by work on I-90 in Cleveland, Ohio where he provided acquisition, relocation and appraisal review services from 1973 through 1975. The company now had offices in Cleveland and Fort Lauderdale. In 1971, he established O. R. Colan Associates, Inc. of West Virginia, "back home" in South Charleston, within walking distance of the house where he had grown up. This location served as corporate headquarters until his death in 1989.

EXPANSION INTO THE AVIATION SECTOR

After World War II, commercial air service was established around the country. By the 1960s, airports began expanding to accommodate the growing aviation industry.

Over the years, ORC played an integral role in building this nation's aviation infrastructure. Like highway expansions, airport construction projects often displace homes and businesses. The Uniform Act of 1970 applied to all federal agencies and any project where federal funding was used. Yet the FAA did not create formal guidelines for its implementation on airport projects until the 1980s.

In 1978, Bob Merryman was working for the Missouri Highway Department when my father hired him to handle an extended approach area acquisition project for the Lambert-St. Louis International Airport. Bob has been with ORC since that time and is currently a Senior Vice President and Director of ORC. The project was being handled internally at the airport, with support by an aviation planning firm. Neither party had experience with land acquisition, so the project was moving slowly. Area residents were complaining that airplane noise was so loud they couldn't sleep. The airport director did not want a hostile public and turned to ORC for advice. The FAA had not yet adopted the use of "Part 150" noise studies to reduce noise in neighborhoods surrounding airports. Those guidelines were not approved until 1981. Prior to that date, airports relied on other rationales for buying property impacted by noise.

Merryman worked with my father and the airport's planning consultant to put together the facts about airplane noise, options for solutions, cost estimates for buying property vs paying damages and recommendations for the best way to proceed. The airport director accepted ORC's recommendations. The buyout was successful, and eventually included more than 5,000 parcels. The real estate was used for two expansion projects, noise buffers and commercial-industrial development.

Lambert-St. Louis International Airport has remained a client of ORC since 1978. In similar fashion, ORC became the consultant of choice for more than 50 airports nationwide. The list includes Cleveland-Hopkins International, Palm Beach International, Providence T. F. Greene International, Seattle-Tacoma International, Chicago O'Hare International, Philadelphia International, Baltimore-Washington International, Orlando Sanford, Little Rock National, Fort Lauderdale-Hollywood International and numerous municipal airports. Some of these airports have been ORC clients for more than 25 years.

Not all projects go smoothly. Public projects that are not welcomed by a community can be especially problematic. This was the case when ORC was hired to handle land acquisition and relocation services for the Seattle-Tacoma Airport's Third Runway Project.

The project manager, Steve Cleary, remembers how environmental protestors damaged heavy equipment at the airport. Then activists found a spotted owl on the airport grounds, strapped themselves to trees and called the media. Meetings with the public were held weekly for 30 weeks. Eventually, the runway was completed, but the relatively straightforward construction project took nearly 19 years from start to finish.

MAKING HISTORY IN TIMES BEACH: ORC'S FIRST FLOOD MITIGATION PROJECT [14]

In the early 1980s, the city of Times Beach, Missouri, was comprised primarily of vacation homes that were increasingly occupied year around. To keep down the dust, the city hired a contractor to spray the unpaved streets. During the week, the contractor used his truck to haul dioxin, a toxic environmental pollutant. On the weekends, he filled it with waste oil to spray the roads. Residual dioxin mixed in with the oil and leached into the ground.

In 1983, two floods spread this hazardous waste across the city, washing contaminated soil into the homes. The Federal Emergency Management Agency (FEMA) ordered the immediate evacuation of more than 250 single-family homes, two mobile home parks and 30 businesses. A total of more than 900 families were displaced by the flood.

The Environmental Protection Agency (EPA) would not allow the city to be reoccupied and ordered FEMA to buy out the residents. Because FEMA had neither the staff nor the knowledge required to purchase so many properties, they hired ORC to do the job.

The Federal Emergency Management Agency (FEMA) funded the Times Beach acquisition and relocation program using funds from the Environmental Protection Agency (EPA) Superfund. However, there were other agencies

---

14 ORC continues to serve communities that are impacted by floods. ORC is currently working for the Governor's Office of Storm Recovery (GOSR) in New York for a temporary relocation program for those impacted by Hurricane Sandy and for a flood mitigation program in North Dakota.

also involved in various aspects of the project. The Times Beach project was fraught with unique situations. The way ORC agents addressed these issues helped secure the company's reputation for excellence in handling complicated acquisitions.

An example of one of the unusual situations involved earlier payments made by the Farmers Home Administration. This agency responded to the initial flood by offering loans with no down-payment to permit tenants to move. However, these same tenants were later determined to be eligible for a down-payment assistance under the Uniform Act provided they actually expended the funds as down-payment. Since no down-payment was required for the Farmers loan, it initially appeared that the tenants had forfeited their eligibility for Uniform Act payments. A local congressman was upset and thought it unfair that the inter-play of two programs resulted in such an unintended consequence. ORC was asked to suggest a solution.

ORC understood the issues, and suggested that an approach we termed "retroactive" down payment would solve the problem. In this solution, the tenant authorized payment of the eligible Uniform Act down-payment funds directly to the lender, thus reducing the loan balance and effectively becoming a down-payment. The requirements of the Uniform Act payment were met, and the tenants gained equity in their new dwellings. It was a good solution.

O. R. COLAN BUILDS A TEAM OF ASSOCIATES

The intensity of the Times Beach project gave the ORC staff many opportunities to bond with each other and with their boss.

"My first day on job, Mr. C. was in the office," remembers Daryl Knobbe. "He was traveling, and took his clothes to the cleaners. He asked me to pick up the order, which included his underwear, but gave me strict instructions not to show it to the girls in the office."

"Mr. C. was tough to get to know," he continues. "Then right before Christmas, he asked me to go shopping with him for his grandchildren, who were 6 and 8 years old. I was only 21. We went to RadioShack, where he tried on a yellow helmet with a red siren. It helped soften his rather proper image and improved our relationship."

Although ORC employees viewed their boss with respect, they enjoyed many memorable times together.

"He loved family dinners and often wanted us to go out together for a big meal at 8 or 9 pm. He didn't have a social life outside of the office, and we were like his family," says Knobbe.

The employees did many fun things together as a group. Sometimes, they would go to one employee's house for dinner and games. "On one occasion, Bob, Daryl, the people from FEMA and I went to a waterslide," remembers Jill Knobbe, who later married Daryl. Both Jill and Daryl have been with ORC Associates now for more than 30 years.

The company purchased an IBM System 21 to help manage the Times Beach project. As ORC's computer programmer at that time, I created a database to track the FEMA payments. Although the company used the latest technology in word processing (the IBM Display Writer), the IBM System 21 was ORC's first real computer. The Times Beach project was also the first project where ORC was asked to have client funds deposited in an escrow account from which we had the authority to draw checks daily.[15]

Over a two-year period, ORC approved payments for more than 900 properties and wrote checks for more than $31 million in FEMA funds. Ten years later, 265,000 tons of contaminated soil were removed and incinerated. In 1999, a 500-acre state park was opened on the site.

The Times Beach project wrapped up just as the Lambert-St. Louis Airport expansion ramped up. Bob Merryman, Daryl Knobbe and Jill Knobbe moved to the airport project and began to add other local clients. Thanks to their good work, ORC has had a solid presence in St. Louis since that time.

---

15 This practice is currently being used on a project in New York City and with work on the California High Speed Rail project, as well as for many of our utility clients where the practice is more common.

Owen Richard Colan was born in Nebraska on December 4, 1922 to Richard Mitchell and Lucille Colan. The family moved to Miami, Florida, and left to return to Nebraska after the hurricane of 1926 and eventually settled in South Charleston, West Virginia, where he graduated from South Charleston High School.

In May of 1941 he posed for this graduation picture when he graduated from West Virginia University with a Degree in Economics.

Owen Richard Colan enlisted in the Naval Air Corps in 1942 and served until the end of World War II in 1945. In 1945 he married Ruth Louis Hillenbrand and entered Georgetown Law School in Washington, D.C. where he earned his J. D. Degree in 1948. Their only child, born in 1948, was named Catherine Louise Colan.

Owen Richard Colan and Ruth Louise Colan in 1945.

The March 25, 1955 edition of the Saturday Evening Post told the story of the new turnpike through West Virginia as told to Richard Thruelson by Dick Colan and others who were interviewed for the article. After my father graduated from Georgetown Law School, his first job was as Chief Right of Way Agent for the West Virginia Turnpike Commission from 1952 – 1957. This is where he began his career in right of way.

Owen Richard Colan is pictured in the center of this picture just behind the front row. As part of his plan to create a right of way department that had the training needed to administer federal funds appropriately and to give every property owner impacted the information they were entitled to, Dick Colan created a training program. Every right of way agent, appraiser and trainee in the West Virginia Right of Way Division completed a detailed course covering the entire text of the AASHO Acquisition for Right of Way course. Pictured here are West Virginia state officials with the Graduating Class of October 3, 1963.

Pictured from left to right are Joe Cohen from the Office of Budget, Owen Richard Colan and Joseph M. O'Connor. Former FBI Agent O'Connor was appointed to direct the new Office of Audit and Investigations of the Bureau of Public Roads as part of a plan to investigate and correct corruption that permeated the highway program prior to that date as reported in the February 4, 1962 edition of Parade Magazine in an investigative article by Jack Anderson entitled "The Great Highway Robbery". Dick Colan had served in the Harrisburg, Pennsylvania office of the Bureau of Public Roads was serving as a Director for the State Road Commission of West Virginia when this picture was taken at the annual AASHTO meeting in December of 1962 in Miami Beach, Florida.

STATE HIGHWAY officials and an industry representative review progress in West Virginia's federal-aid highway program with Sen. Jennings Randolph, D-W. Va., chairman of the Senate Public Works Committee. Seated with Randolph is Joseph Speed Jones, Charleston highway engineer. Also pictured are (from left) O. R. Colan, director of the State Road Commission's right-of-way division; Earl R. Seyoc, director of the construction division; and Eugene H. Brown, executive director of The Associated General Contractors of West Virginia, Inc., all of Charleston.

SRC RIGHT-OF-WAY 'NERVE CENTER'—This is the "nerve center" of the right-of-way division of the SRC. Philip P. Joseph, assistant director, foreground, keeps in touch with each property transaction in the state. Keying him in on a recent development is Mrs. Okey Reed Jr., control room operator. The charts record each step the state takes in buying property for right-of-way for state and interstate highways.—Daily Mail Photo by Earl Benton.

O. R. COLAN
Right of Way Chief

Colan Heads Right of Way

O. R. (Dick) Colan of South Charleston, who has been a right of way officer in West Virginia for the U. S. Bureau of Public R o a d s, has been appointed to head the State Road Commission's newly-created right of way division.

Colan has an impressive background in the field of right of way acquisition. Before working with the U. S. bureau's West Virginia division, he held a similar post with the Pennsylvania division, and formerly was chief right of way man for the West Virginia Turnpike Commission and assistant chief right of way agent for the State Road Commission.

A native of Lincoln, Neb., Colan attended public schools in South Charleston, attended Bethany College, and earned a bachelor of arts degree at West Virginia University before taking a law degree at Georgetown University.

Road Commissioner Burl Sawyers said Colan's appointment is part of an announced plan to re-

Sunday Gazette-Mail, Charleston, WV, November 11, 1962.

Owen Richard Colan, J.D. pictured in 1966 at his desk as Director of Right of Way of the West Virginia Department of Highways in Charleston, West Virginia.

In 1969 my father left his job with the West Virginia Department of Highways to open the first company called O. R. Colan Associates of Florida, Inc. which was soon followed by O. R. Colan Associates, Inc. of WV. His marketing strategy was based on creating and instructing courses based on The Uniform Relocation Assistance and Real Property Acquisition Policies Act of 1970 (Uniform Act), the administrative law that forms the basis of our technical expertise. He is pictured here teaching one of those early courses. He was greatly admired for his teaching skills. My introduction to the technical side of our business was as the editor of the textbooks that he wrote.

This picture was taken around 1985 and is one of the last formal pictures of Dick Colan prior to his death in 1989.

Catherine Colon Muth   *Libby Braley Colan*   *Fran LaMonica*

Libby and Fran owned stock in O. R. Colan Associates that the company repurchased as Treasury Stock by 1993. My father was widowed in 1973 and remarried Libby Braley in 1989 just months before his death.

Above: O. R. Colan Associates was named among the Top Fifty Women Led Businesses in Florida from 2005 through 2015 by The Commonwealth Institute. The award is based on gross revenues. I am pictured here receiving the award for ORC in 2015.

Above left: In 1996, I was nominated by BB&T to participate in the Entrepreneur of the Year program sponsored by Earnst & Young. I am pictured to the left as a Finalist with another finalist, Joe Jeffries, Jr. At the time, O. R. Colan Associates had 80 employees.

Right: In March of 2000, AASHTO invited me to represent the private right of way sector as part of the European Right-of-Way and Utilities Scan Tour. The Scanning Study Team visited four European countries to share beat practices. The countries in the study included Norway, Germany, the Netherlands and the United Kingdom. Pictured above from left to right are the member of the Study Team: Richard Moeller, FHWA Team

Leader; Joachim Pestinger, Washington State DOT, Team Leader; Adele McCormick, Report Facilitator; Catherine Colan Muth, O. R. Colan Associates; Stuart Waymack, Virginia DOT (standing); Myron Frierson, Michigan DOT (sitting); Janet Myers, Maine DOT; Wayne Kennedy, International Right of Way Association; and Paul Scott, FHWA.

... inspiring confidence in progress

Owen Richard Colan, J.D., was a native of South Charleston and proud to be a West Virginian. After serving in the Naval Air Corps during World War II, he earned a law degree from Georgetown Law School. His career in right of way began after law school with the West Virginia Turnpike where he acquired land for the two lane version of the WV Turnpike.

Dick Colan served in the Federal Highway Administration's Harrisburg, Pennsylvania office from 1960 until 1962 and returned to West Virginia as Director of Right of Way in 1963 where he restructured and reformed the Right of Way Division of the WV Department of Transportation. In 1969 he established O. R. Colan Associates which proudly remains a testimony to his vision for using consultants for the right of way phase of highway construction.

We at O. R. Colan Associates invite you to enjoy your visit to this beautiful state!

ORC O.R.Colan ASSOCIATES
REAL ESTATE SOLUTIONS FOR INFRASTRUCTURE
704.529.3115 • www.orcolan.com

Above: In 2014 the annual IRWA Conference was held in Charleston, West Virginia. ORC was asked to do a Special Sponsorship in Memory of my father. This full page ad appeared in the Program for the event.

Right: I am pictured here with the plaque that IRWA presented to ORC at the conference in Memory of Mr. Colan for his service as the Director of Right of Way for the West Virginia Department of Highways from 1962 – 1969.

In August of 2016 the Leadership Team of ORC met in Columbus, Ohio for a 2-day planning meeting. Pictured from left to right are Richie McNally, Daryl Knobbe, Carmen Johnson, Cathy Muth, Tracy Jones, Steve Toth, Steve Chastain and Karen Ammar.

Pictured above center is Tasha Ethridge of Collins Elementary School, winner of the 2014 Catherine Muth Academic and Citizenship Award. She is flanked by Mr. Jackie Ford, Collins Elementary Community Liaison, and Cathy Muth.

Pictured below is the Peace Garden donated by ORC to Virginia Shuman Young Montessori Elementary School in Fort Lauderdale, Florida. Felicity Harris, a 2006 student at VSY is shown here in the Peace Garden.

In 2003 we reorganized the company, changing from a "C" Corporation to a Limited Liability Company. Pictured here with Cathy are her children and co-owners of the company, Karen Ammar (left) and Kevin Ammar (right). Karen is the Chairman of ORC. Kevin is a medical doctor and not active in the business.

Women in business understand how important it is to have a supportive husband. My husband Fred has encouraged and supported me for more than three decades. We are pictured here in 2015. Fred retired in 2008 from his Bluefield, West Virginia law firm of Hensley, Muth, Garton & Hayes where he represented coal miners in black lung cases, social security disability and worker's comp. He is also widely known and loved for his roles on the stage of Summit Players.

Fred has a gift for making me laugh. In 1989 right after my father passed I was in the Fort Lauderdale office trying to get my head around all that had to be done. I called him on night and complained "I can't even find the corporate seal!" to which he responded "He is probably swimming in the ocean." I needed that.

Together we have ten beautiful grandchildren.

PART II
THE SECOND GENERATION
1989 - 2016

Chapter 5

THE MANTLE OF LEADERSHIP PASSES

On April 6, 1989, my father and Ted Pluta were on their way to make a presentation for the St. Lucie (Florida) International Airport when they stopped for breakfast. My father told Ted he didn't feel well, and suggested that Ted might need to make some of the presentation. "He said this all the time, but then he'd get on a roll and do the whole presentation," says Pluta.

That's exactly what happened that day. But later the same evening, my father suffered a severe heart attack. He was taken to a hospital in Hollywood, Florida, where he valiantly continued to direct his company's operations. Two days later, on April 8, he suffered another heart attack. This one was fatal.

As is often the case with businesses run by a founder and visionary, succession planning was never discussed. My father's death left the employees in shock. They wondered whether the firm would continue, and if it did, how would they manage without their leader?

"Mr. C. was the ship. No one thought about what we would do without him," says Steve Cleary, a real estate appraiser hired in 1986. "He was our founder, president, voice and proposal writer. We wondered who would chase proposals, how would we find and recruit people, where would we be in five years. There was a huge void when he left."

"It will take several heads to make some of the decisions that he would have made," said Bob Gallion in my father's obituary published in the Fort Lauderdale *Sun-Sentinel* on April 10, 1989.

I remember seeing the distraught faces of the managers who gathered around the conference table after my father's funeral. They all looked directly at me as if to say, "Okay, you're in charge now. What do you want us to do?" It was the moment I realized the mantle had been given to me. It was my responsibility to sustain the company and continue the work that my father had begun. I remember feeling like I was in the control seat of a fast moving train, and all I could do was hold on.

During this time, I doubted my own ability to lead the company. I called Bob Merryman in desperation one night and begged him to be President of the company. He just laughed and said, "Oh, you can do it, Cathy. I'll help you but I don't want to be President." I had no choice but to carry on.

At the time of my father's death, many of our senior level managers had been with the company for 10 years or more. He kept a tight rein on his employees. I gave them more authority over day-to-day activities. It was the right business decision, but it was more out of necessity than a strategic decision. They had more knowledge of the technical side of the business than I did. I had worked as editor of the courses my father had developed and served as the company's computer programmer. My knowledge was on the corporate administrative side.

Allowing senior managers more autonomy served ORC well in the immediate years following my father's untimely death.

Steve Cleary was one of the senior-level managers at the time. He recalls many talks with me about my vision for the company, how to attract better staff and the importance of providing staff with the tools to succeed. "Cathy was open to new ideas. She understood the importance of empowering her managers. Over the years she surrounded herself with some really good people, and she gave us room to work through problems and find solutions," he says.

"I do not always agree with her decisions, but she is the one taking the risks," he continues. "She put her heart and soul into this company. I am proud to say that I had a small part in the success of ORC, but it has been a group effort."

THE FINANCIAL CHALLENGES OF TRANSITION

In 1980, my father made O. R. Colan Associates of Florida, Inc., a wholly owned subsidiary of O. R. Colan Associates, Inc. of West Virginia. This greatly simplified his estate in advance of his passing. Yet he died without a will, leaving many challenges for his heirs. My mother had died in 1973, and he had remained a widower for 16 years before marrying his long-time co-worker Elizabeth (Libby) Braley only months before his death. Because he died intestate, two-thirds of his personal property, including his stock in O. R. Colan Associates, Inc. of West Virginia went to me as his only child, and one-third went to his wife. Libby and I were already stockholders, and the event left me with majority control. Over the next two years, I purchased the remaining stock from Libby and the only other stockholder, Fran LaMonica.

My challenges began one week after my father's death, when our bank cancelled ORC's line of credit. I had been in touch with the bank for several days preceding the first payroll after his death to tell them I might need to use our line of credit to meet payroll. After the payroll was processed that Friday, I called the bank to say I would need $50,000 to cover the payroll. The bank responded by saying they had decided to withdraw ORC's line of credit. I said "You realize this action will end our banking relationship?" and they said, "Yes." They refused to budge. I cashed in a $50,000 life insurance policy I received from my father's estate to cover payroll. It was the only life insurance I had received.

A line of credit was essential, because government agencies are slow to pay, and while the company had a substantial accounts receivable balance, there was no cash in the bank to make payroll or pay other ongoing expenses. The following week, as the new chief executive officer of ORC, I approached four other banks in Charleston for a line of credit and, to my dismay, was turned down. The bankers were polite but very condescending. They told me that, historically, second-generation business owners do not have a good chance of succeeding. It was also clear that they had no faith that a woman could succeed in business.

All four banks requested an interim financial statement, but we were behind in our bookkeeping. I was reluctant to pay the $10,000 fee that an accounting firm would charge to generate an interim financial statement.

Fortunately, the future of ORC was assured with the fifth bank I approached. Phyllis Arnold, then president of One Valley Bank, was a friend of mine from West Virginia University. The loan officer I met with was also a woman. They were the first women I encountered in my banking visits. When the bank asked for an interim statement, this time I had learned my lesson and found the money needed to meet that requirement. One Valley Bank gave ORC a line of credit, and ORC has remained with this bank (and its successor, BB&T) ever since. Today, we are one of their larger clients in that region.

ORC PROVES IT CAN SURVIVE

The effort my father placed into hiring and training top agents secured ORC a reputation for excellence that enabled the company to survive and grow after its founder's death.

I remember the first proposal we won after my father's passing. We submitted a proposal to the Federal Highway Administration to develop a training course for the National Highway Institute, its training arm. We really did not know if we could win work without my father, because he was such an important part of our company. When we were awarded this first project, I danced on the ceiling! It proved that we could win work without our founder. It was a huge milestone for us.

Obtaining new contracts for right of way business requires developing and maintaining relationships. ORC managers network with individuals from city governments and engineering firms to keep ORC in the forefront of their clients' minds. Most managers work in their home territory, which enables them to maintain ongoing contact with customers.

"We are there when the client needs us," says Bob Merryman. "Our business has grown by word of mouth. We have a lot of repeat clients, because they are happy with us, hire us again and recommend us to other municipalities."

ORC'S AIRPORT ERA

Based on the solid reputation established by the ORC team at the Lambert-St. Louis International Airport, ORC continued to win work on airport projects in other locations. Noise mitigation and expansion programs at airports in St. Louis, Fort Lauderdale, West Palm Beach, Cleveland, Seattle and Toledo as well as at smaller municipal airports proved to be our strongest area of growth in the decade after my father's passing.

In 1989 the Toledo Lucas County Port Authority hired ORC to acquire 200 homes in close proximity to the runway and assist with the relocation process. Steve Cleary was a senior agent in the Fort Lauderdale office and I asked him if he would like to manage this airport project for ORC. "After discussing with Cathy Muth, I saw this as a great opportunity for advancement" says Cleary. "Cathy and Bob Merryman were both very supportive and Toledo was a great success which allowed ORC to get more work in the Midwest. We also picked up airport land acquisition projects in Cleveland and Dayton Ohio and some LPA projects in the region."

Steve Toth was hired by ORC after graduation from college in 1992. He remembers being part of the site survey team for the Cleveland-Hopkins project where our dedicated staff worked in below-zero temperatures to meet with residents at the beginning of that project. When Steve Cleary accepted a new position as Project Manager for ORC's Seattle-Tacoma International Airport project in 1994, Steve Toth moved to Cleveland from the Toledo Express Airport project to serve as Project Manager for the Cleveland-Hopkins noise mitigation program. A total of 470 parcels were acquired over the next 8 years, along with a self-storage facility that was acquired for a runway extension in 2001. Mr. Toth managed the ongoing program at that airport for more than a dozen years before moving into his current role as the company's Chief Operating Officer in 2006.

During the noise mitigation program, a 10-year dispute ensued between the City of Cleveland and the City of Brook Park over expansion of the airport and removal of the International Exposition Center, a 1940s factory used to build bombers during World War II that had been converted into a convention and trade show center. The IX Center was located in Brook Park adjacent to the airport. The City of Cleveland was trying to add another runway to accommodate the increased traffic associated with Continental Airlines establishing a regional hub in Cleveland. In 2001 the two cities reached a settlement agreement that allowed Cleveland to move forward with expansion. In exchange, Cleveland would alter its city boundaries to put the NASA Glenn Research Center in Brook Park. As part of the settlement agreement, an additional 248 residential properties were purchased for the airport.

ORC is still providing services after more than 22 consecutive years, currently holding an on-call appraisal services contract with the Cleveland-Hopkins International Airport.

FEDERAL AGENCY CLIENTS

Over the years, ORC has worked on a wide variety of projects for a diverse assortment of clients that include the FHWA, EPA, FAA, U. S. Army Corps of Engineers (USACE), Department of Housing and Urban Development (HUD) and the National Park Service (NPS), among other agencies. Some assignments have been memorable.

The following article from ORC's newsletter, *The Acquirer*, describes how the company assisted the NPS with relocation for the memorial to Flight 93.

The tragedy of September 11, 2001, had many faces. Most people can remember where they were when the saw or heard about the incident at the World Trade Center in New York. And we all recall the additional carnage that followed with a crash at the Pentagon and the crash of Flight 93 that was heading towards the Capitol. Due to the actions of the passengers on Flight 93, that plane never reached its target, but instead crashed in rural Pennsylvania. Shortly thereafter, Congress designated a memorial to be built at the crash site. The opening date of the Memorial is planned for the tenth anniversary on September 11, 2011, to commemorate the bravery of these ordinary people who potentially saved hundreds of lives.

What does the Flight 93 Memorial have to do with relocation? The designated area is about 2000 acres, and encompasses the actual crash site. While we might picture the rural site as vacant, it was actually surrounded by improved uses. There were homes and businesses near the actual site. These were acquired for the development of the Memorial.

Since Federal funds were being used for the development of the park, all of the land acquisition was in compliance with the Uniform Act. And, any person required to move from the site was afforded relocation payments and services. One of those displaced persons was a large scrap metal business.

Like many agencies, the National Park Service only occasionally encounters a large business move. As such, they opted to seek consultant services to assist them with their effort. ORC provided assistance in the preparation, and solicitation of moving bids. We also assisted NPS in the evaluation of alternative relocation payments to expeditiously move the project forward in order to maintain the schedule. The move is now underway; construction is ready; and come September 2011, there will be a new fitting memorial for all those persons who gave up their lives on Flight 93.

ORC also helped the NPS relocate the tenants of Boston's famous Faneuil Hall prior to renovation in 2010, as explained in this article *The Acquirer*:

Faneuil Hall, built in 1742, was used as a marketplace and meeting hall. It was the site of various Revolutionary War speeches and has taken center stage in American politics. In 1979, it was the backdrop for Ted Kennedy's presidential campaign announcement, and in 2004, the site of John Kerry's concession speech.

Periodically in its 250-year life, the building was expanded and modernized. In 2010, the landmark needed extensive renovation. The National Park Service felt it would be best for tenants to vacate the property during the work period and hired ORC to provide relocation services. Because the National Park Service had no way to pay for relocation expenses, they gave ORC the funds, which were put into a trust account. This allowed ORC to issue reimbursement checks directly to the tenants.

ORC agents work hard at integrating into the community to help ease the pain of relocation. The team working on Faneuil Hall set about building relationships with the business owners by asking who had the best lobster rolls. Everyone was eager to share their opinion, and the team enjoyed sampling multiple sandwiches from various shops. In no time at all, the relocation work was completed, and renovations could begin.

PROJECT MANAGEMENT OVERSIGHT FOR TRANSIT

ORC has been the right of way partner on numerous project management oversight teams for federal transit projects.

The Federal Transit Administration (FTA) provides federal funding for various transit projects throughout the nation. Because the FTA has limited staff, it retains project management oversight contract (PMOC) specialists to assist with oversight of the transit agencies that actually implement these projects. ORC has been subcontracted by various large engineering firms to provide expert real estate acquisition and relocation assistance services on a dozen or more FTA transit projects since the early 2000s.

One of these assignments was for the Central Subway Project in San Francisco, California. In this case, ORC served as a subcontractor to STV Incorporated.

A major challenge was the project's location in the congested parts of San Francisco known as Chinatown and South of Market Street (SoMa), where the Moscone Conference Center is situated. The Moscone Center Station parcel housed three commercial businesses. The Chinatown Station location had 19 apartment units on the second floor and eight retail tenants on the ground floor. The Chinatown Community Development Center (CCDC) was retained to assist ORC in working with the community. CCDC staff acted as translators and interpreters to ensure that affected occupants understood the process and were given full assistance in accordance with program requirements.

THE DESIGN-BUILD SECTOR

ORC recognized that states were moving to adopt the design build model or Public Private Partnerships (PPP) for building highways. Our company was the right of way provider on some of the first of these projects including the Pocahontas Parkway in Virginia and the Veterans Expressway in Florida. We were the right of way consultant for both phases of the SH 130 project in Austin, Texas; for Sections 1-5 of the Grand Parkway in Houston, Texas; and for the Route 158 Design Build project in North Carolina.

At one time most of our revenue was from airport projects, but more recently the largest projects won have been in the design build sector. These projects are very schedule driven and require large, fully dedicated teams. They have a very long lead time and require years of planning before the right of way phase begins.

WATER/WASTEWATER

In recent years many municipalities have been under Consent Decrees wherein a court ordered them to make improvements to their water and wastewater systems to prevent backflow from the sewer systems into public water systems during periods of heavy rainfall. ORC has worked with a number of municipalities to purchase the land or easements needed for these improvements. In 2016 we created a Water/Wastewater Division to pursue future work in this area.

FLOOD MITIGATION PROGRAMS

Our first flood mitigation program was a contract with FEMA in the early 1980s to buy the entire city of Times Beach, Missouri after a flood washed soil contaminated with dioxin into the homes along the riverbank.

More recently we developed policies and procedures for the Governor's Office of Storm Recovery in the State of New York for a temporary relocation program funded by HUD to allow people to move temporarily while their homes were retrofitted after Hurricane Sandy. One of my goals in participating in this program was to be ready to help other states in a timely manner when federal funding is granted to a state for disaster recovery efforts. Since disasters only occur occasionally, it is hard for a state to understand the complexities of administering the federal funds that are given to the state.

Often these arrive in the form of Community Development Grand funds to be administered on the County level. Our goal is to help these agencies deliver benefits to those impacted as quickly as possible after one of these events.

ORC TRAINING

In 2001 we formed a separate company for training and research. This company was rolled into O. R. Colan Associates, LLC in 2016. The ORC Training Division is led by Lisa Barnes as Vice President of Training. Bob Merryman is part of this division along with a number of part time technical experts who are retired heads of the real estate divisions of FHWA (Dick Moeller), FTA (Ron Fannin), HUD (Joan Morgan), FHWA Division Office Retirees (Bob Kleinburd and Charles O'Neill). The technical expertise of these individuals is unequalled by our competitors. These experts have created courses and articles available to all employees through the ORC Knowledge Base.

In 2015 we signed a licensing agreement with IRWA to put eight of our internal training courses into their online platform. These courses were designed as part of the curriculum of our Jr. Agent training program. Our goal was to put these in an online format so that it would be economical to deliver this training to our Jr. Agents and other employees. The licensing agreement with IRWA takes this a step further by offering the courses to others outside of our company. We believe this is an important contribution to our industry.

Our training division has also completed several research studies for FHWA. The approach to conducting the research depends on the purpose or goal of the study or project, and the parameters outlined by the client.

* In 2010-2011, we completed a *Business Relocation Retrospective Study* to assess the adequacy of the current statutory limits for reestablishment expenses and nonresidential fixed payments. The team recommended an increase in these payment limits and a provision for inflation adjustments to any new limits in the Uniform Act and the implementing regulations. The MAP-21 amendments to the Uniform Act, effective October 1, 2014, did increase the statutory limits for

both payments, and included language that the lead agency, FHWA, can make adjustments to the amounts of these payments based on cost of living, inflation or other factors.

* The *Reverse Mortgages in Relocation Assistance Study* performed in 2011-2012, provided the FHWA with the technical expertise on reverse mortgages needed to develop guidance for establishing a fair and effective method of addressing reverse mortgages when displacing persons in accordance with the Uniform Act.

* Another research study, *Process Streamlining: Notices and Offers by Electronic Methods* (2013-2014) furnished the FHWA with the technical information necessary to determine how internet-based systems can be used to streamline the acquisition process, and how they can assist in the delivery of notices and offers that are integral to the ROW process.

* We completed the *Option Contracts Research Study* in 2015, which reviewed and evaluated the use of option contracts in Federally-funded advance acquisition projects. Some of the findings from this research study may be beneficial to future research efforts into standardizing and improving implementation of state and federally-funded early acquisition provisions.

Studies like these are often done by FHWA as the foundation of potential changes to the law and regulations. ORC is a leading provider of these kinds of research studies for FHWA and other federal agencies.

ORC UTILITY & INFRASTRUCTURE LAND SERVICES, LLC

ORC occasionally provided services to utility companies in areas where we had established offices like St. Louis and Cleveland, but O. R. Colan Associates was so well known and branded for the work we were doing in the public transportation sectors that it was hard to convince utility clients that we could serve their needs as well. When we called on potential utility clients we were greeted with statements like "Oh, yes. We know you. You are the airport people." Or, "You work on highway projects." So, in 2010, we formed ORC Utility & Infrastructure Land Services, LLC (ORC U&I) to help rebrand ourselves for the utility sector. The new company was slow to get started until we found the right leader in Richie McNally who is now our Vice President of ORC Utility & Infrastructure and a member of our Leadership Team. In 2015 this company provided 30% of our revenue and continues to grow under Richie's leadership.

Rebuilding our country's electric grid and the new pipelines needed to connect new sources of energy to our energy grid has become the nation's "new interstate transportation system", comparable to the Interstate Highway System of the 1960s. This new interstate transportation system is critically needed for energy rather than for cars. Just as the building of our interstate highway system was an important part of our national defense system, this energy transportation system is now what is needed to make our country economically strong, secure and independent. This is the decade for opportunity in this sector and we are working to position ORC U&I as the preferred provider for utility clients nationwide.

HOW VISTAGE IMPACTED OUR SUCCESS

In 1996, I joined The Executive Committee (TEC) Group 2004, which was later renamed Vistage. This international community of CEOs has local chapters that meet monthly. Mornings are dedicated to a speaker. In the afternoons, participants present issues and receive input and recommendations from the group.

Vistage has been a key factor in ORC's success. In my more than 20 years of membership, Vistage exposed me to hundreds of experts in critical areas of leadership. The topics we covered gave me a broader and deeper understanding of business issues. Many attorneys and other experts we use as consultants were introduced to me through Vistage. The Vistage experience enabled me to have a bigger vision for our company.

Part of the Vistage experience is having a Chair who facilitates meetings and serves as a personal business coach to the members. My Chair for

20 years was Tom Foster, who is recognized as one of the best Chairs in the organization.

In 2000, I used Vistage as a sounding board, raising the challenges of communicating with teams located in multiple cities around the nation. By then, ORC had more than 100 employees in 29 offices in 20 states, with those numbers changing from month to month as projects closed and new projects began.

It became clear that the methods of communication that worked when ORC was a smaller company—primarily one-on-one conversations—were no longer sufficient for a company that was spread out in many locations. With the help of my Vistage group, I began to focus on solutions for ORC's communication issues. We created a communication plan that went far beyond the traditional meeting setting. We created both an internal (The Business Update) and external newsletter (The Acquirer) as well as bi-annual Town Hall Meetings held over the internet using Skype. In-person meetings are still important in building relationships, but we realize that ongoing communication can be achieved effectively using technology. Recently, we added Yammer, an internal Facebook-style site, as a communication tool.

Our Vistage participation has expanded to include other members of the ORC Leadership Team. The ongoing training and sharing of information and challenges with other business leaders continues to be important to our growth as individual leaders and as a company.

Chapter 6

● ● ●

THE COMPANY AND ITS CEO MATURE

In 2000, Dick Moeller was Director of the Real Estate Services Division at the FHWA's Washington headquarters and secretary of AASHTO's Right of Way and Utilities Subcommittee. AASHTO, FHWA and the Transportation Research Board (TRB) arranged a tour of selected European countries to identify best practices in right of way acquisition and relocation that could be applied in the U.S. They called this the European Right of Way and Utilities Scan Tour.

Moeller and a colleague decided it would be a good idea to invite someone along to represent private consultants. Moeller had become acquainted with me, because ORC traditionally hosted the opening reception of AASHTO's annual meeting. He extended the invitation to me to represent the private side of the right of way industry on the tour.

When I received the invitation. I was working on several proposals and did not think I could spare the time. I asked Bob Merryman to represent the company, but he encouraged me to go. It was a decision I never regretted.

The Scan Tour was significant, because it gave me the opportunity to get to know several people at FHWA and at state DOTs, who subsequently became lifelong friends. These included Dick Moeller, Paul Scott and others who have since retired. It also gave me the opportunity to be published and to participate on panels at the AASHTO annual meetings and at the International Right of Way Association's Annual Conference.

The team representing the United States on the Scan Tour included right of way directors from Maine, Michigan, Virginia and Washington State; two representatives from the FHWA; two from the private sector; a professional writer and a guide.[16] We visited Norway, Germany, the United Kingdom and the Netherlands.

In addition to right of way acquisition and relocation, the international professionals discussed practices pertaining to appraisal waivers, appraisal review modification, early right of way acquisition, corridor preservation, land consolidation and other aspects of the right of way process.

Every country was eager to exchange information. We were continually surprised by the number of similarities between our program implemented under the Uniform Act and the programs administered in the four European countries we visited. We had all created similar processes, although we had taken different paths. This realization affirmed that our intentions and methods were essentially right and universal. The full report entitled *European Right-of-Way and Utilities Best Practices* is available on FHWA's website at http://international.fhwa.dot.gov/eurorightofway/index.cfm.

Ten days into the tour, my feelings of excitement changed when I received news that my grandmother, who was living with us at the time, suffered a major heart attack. Heartbroken, I flew home immediately. I was very close to my grandmother. My mother had died when I was 23, and I was the only grandchild on my father's side.

My grandmother surprised everyone by sitting up to greet me when I arrived and introducing me to all the nurses. She died the following day with me by her side.

The Scan Tour prompted the formation of an Implementation Task Group comprised of the original Scan Team members, plus others from the various state departments of transportation and the private sector. The group identified potential areas where processes could be improved by adapting some of

---

16 Moeller, FHWA Team Leader; Joachim Pestinger, Washington State DOT, Team Leader; Adele McCormick, Report Facilitator; Catherine Colan Muth, O. R. Colan Associates; Stuart Waymack, Virginia DOT; Myron Frierson, Michigan DOT; Janet Myers, Maine DOT; Wayne Kennedy, International Right of Way Association; and Paul Scott, FHWA.

the practices we observed in Europe and various pilot projects were initiated across the nation with cooperating state departments of transportation.

One key finding was that right of way professionals in Europe were trained at the college level. Norway had a five-year degree program specifically for the right of way field. The Implementation Task Group seized this concept as a potential solution to a 2001 finding by FHWA's National Highway Institute (NHI) indicating an impending shortage of trained right of way personnel in the U.S. The shortage occurred as a long-term result of state budgets that cut or eliminated DOT-sponsored training programs, reduced the number of right of way personnel and froze hiring. It also reflected the retirement of experienced right of way personnel.

Additionally, the pressure to shift responsibility for right of way to the local level increased the volume of work performed by local public agencies—work that was previously handled by state personnel.

"Approximately 20,000 local public agencies in the United States had staff that may not have been prepared to administer the land acquisition and relocation phases of a public project," says Dick Moeller. "This clearly indicated a serious need for emphasis on training."

The Scan Tour Implementation Task Group began working with the FHWA to establish a college-level curriculum that would prepare students for a career in the right of way profession at colleges designated as National Transportation Centers. To date, that effort has met with limited success.

Although the Implementation Task Force disbanded in 2003, I continue to seek ways to create a career path for the next generation of right of way experts. I believe the solution ultimately resides in distance learning. In 2015, ORC signed a landmark licensing agreement for ORC Training to develop online courses that qualify for IRWA certifications and continuing education credits. This paves the way for quality online courses that will be available not only to ORC employees, but also to right of way agents worldwide.

THE LEADERSHIP STRUCTURE EVOLVES

By 2000, ORC had grown to 100 employees, yet retained a flat organizational structure. The senior managers acted as our advisory board and reported directly to me. I decided to build an executive team that would ensure the future of the company and eventually allow it to be professionally managed with family members serving on the Board of Directors.

At the time, I was wearing multiple hats, including those of proposal writer, information technology (IT) director, human resources manager, business development manager, chief operating officer, president and CEO. Barbara Saathoff served as my personal assistant and good friend. Some days Barbara would decide that I was getting too stressed and would put a Dairy Queen sundae in front of me. If things got really stressful, we would joke that we were having a two-sundae day. Once she made me go shopping for an hour, just to relax. Another time she came and gently pushed my right shoulder down. I was holding it against my ear as I often did when holding the phone with my shoulder, but without the phone.

I read somewhere that once a company grew to 100 employees, it was time to hire a full-time human resources professional, so I decided to make that position the first addition to our professional management team. My office staff questioned the decision. "What are they going to do that we aren't already doing?" they asked. I told them that if I knew the answer, I would teach them how to do it. It was time to add people who knew more about human resources and other areas than I did.

I asked a friend in human resources (Maria Ferrante, who later married Ed Wilson) to review and shortlist three candidates. I hired the first person I interviewed after only five minutes, because I had to get to the airport. "The job is yours if you will accept it," I said. She was flabbergasted because she was aware that you should take care in the interview process to select the right candidate. But I depended heavily on intuition for new hires, and I felt she was the right person for the job. Her name was Kathy Rupar, and she managed our Human Resources for 10 years.

The next position filled was that of chief financial officer (CFO). We were less successful in selecting the first few CFOs. They were good people, but their unfamiliarity with government contracting made them a poor fit for our company. In 2001, I finally got the right CFO in place and began to build an Executive Team to lead the company. We hired a proposal writer in 2000, followed by an IT director in 2002. The senior managers urged me to create a chief operating officer (COO) position, and I selected Steve Toth, one of our senior managers, to fill that role in 2006. Steve was an excellent choice for the position, because he had technical knowledge of our industry, the respect of his peers and, most importantly, his decisions were very much in line with my own thinking.

By 2006, ORC's first Executive Team was in place. It consisted of the CEO, President, COO, CFO and Vice President of Human Resources.

In 2008, two senior managers were added to improve communication with field offices. They were Daryl Knobbe, who had been with ORC for more than 20 years, and Keith Shepherd, a relatively new hire with a mortgage brokerage background. We chose Keith for his ability to bring us ideas from outside our industry.

Soon thereafter, unfortunately, the role of the Executive Team changed from one of managing the company's growth to managing its downsizing—or "right-sizing." The recession had a dramatic impact on ORC, causing business to drop 30 percent over the prior year.

One loss was the ARC Tunnel Project between New York and New Jersey, which New Jersey Governor Chris Christie canceled in 2010. ORC was in charge of relocation on both sides of the river. The project was expected to bring in $1 million in annual revenue, and ORC had been working on it for nearly a year when it was canceled.

The ARC Tunnel was one of three significant contracts that were canceled in a space of 30 days. At that point, it became clear ORC would have to make cuts to survive. Letting employees go was very difficult for us. We were inclined to hold on to people out of loyalty when they were in between assignments. But at an Executive Team meeting in 2010, I told my team I would not stand in the way of making hard decisions. I told them "My father gave me very little business advice, but he told me long ago that if times should ever get tough, I should not hesitate to let people go. He said that he held onto employees too long in the downturn of the 1980s, and it almost cost him the company."

We made company-wide cuts that included both the Vice President of Human Resources and the CFO. Over a two-year period, the number of employees fell from 140 to 80. It was painful, but necessary. We were cutting muscle.

THE EXECUTIVE TEAM BECOMES THE ORC LEADERSHIP TEAM

In reaction to the Great Recession, a new Executive Team emerged, comprised of the CEO, President, COO, Vice President of Project Development and Vice President of Business Development, with the Controller acting as an advisor.

The team developed a strategic plan focusing on business development. We understood it takes up to two years to build relationships with potential clients. We identified groups of clients where we believed future opportunities lay and began the process of building those relationships.

By 2012, the strategic plan succeeded, and ORC was able to shift its focus from business development to recruiting. In the first seven months of 2013, ORC hired 37 new employees, growing the business back to 125. Recruitment continues today, with the total number of employees in mid-2016 standing at 155.

This series of events taught me a valuable lesson: We learned that business goes in cycles, so we can expect there will be both ups and downs in our future. Today, we are better able to manage in both good and bad times.

In 2013, the Executive Team was renamed the Leadership Team to better describe its role.

PRICE AND COST ARE NOT THE SAME

Failure to understand the right of way process can be a costly mistake.

Unfortunately, many clients look at the cost of each element of a project separately, assuming that if they keep individual costs down, the cost of the project will be lower. But it doesn't work that way. Clients are more likely to achieve their goal if they consider the total cost of a project, which may include the cost of delays, putting more parcels into condemnation or public image issues that can occur when a consultant is not qualified to perform the work.

Sometimes, a lower unit price comes with the condition that limited contacts be made with each owner. This can lead to a higher number of parcels that are not settled amicably and, consequently, higher costs involved in condemning those parcels.

ORC's ability to survive and thrive requires the ongoing education of potential clients at all levels, from local and state agencies to engineers and attorneys.

"If you don't understand right of way, you won't be able to meet the construction schedule, and you will lose money," says Steve Cleary. "Many sponsors do not understand the services we provide and hire the lowest bidder, rather than the most qualified one. We fight for recognition as professionals. That is why establishing relationships with clients and sponsors is so important," he says.

Government agencies like to use consultants that provide turnkey services. They prefer to assign projects to companies that can manage the project, acquire the right of way and relocate people and businesses. Sometimes, these are engineering firms. Other times, an engineering firm will subcontract the acquisition work to a right of way company that conducts the appraisals and acquires the properties. That doesn't always mean the engineers understand right of way, however, as ORC's experience bidding on the South Florida Water Management District's (SFWMD) Comprehensive Everglades Restoration Plan (the CERP) clearly illustrates.

When Dick Moeller joined ORC directly after his retirement from FHWA, he flew to Palm Beach, where he joined ORC's land acquisition team in bidding on the SFWMD project as subcontractors to an engineering firm.

I remember practicing for the presentation. The team, which was comprised primarily of engineers, proposed a plan for storing water. ORC was allocated only five minutes of the 30-minute presentation. We rehearsed all day.

Our brief presentation included the statement that "This will be a high-profile, federally funded program," I said. "It will be imperative to follow the Uniform Act in acquiring land to ensure that $8.4 billion[17] in federal funding will not be at risk."

At one point, the lead engineer came over to the ORC team and said, "Look, I know you think the Uniform Act is important, but maybe we should ask an expert." Dick and I were flabbergasted. Who would we ask? If Dick Moeller, who had just retired from his position as Program Manager for the

---

17 The program was never fully funded. As of 2015 just over $1 billion in federal and $1 billion in state funds have been allocated to the project according to an article in the April 27, 2016 edition of the Sun Sentinel by Jason Kirk, Commander of the Jacksonville office of the U. S. Army Corps of Engineers entitled *Everglades Restoration Projects Already Showing Benefits.*

Office of Real Estate Services at FHWA, the "lead agency" in Washington, DC and one of the authors of the Uniform Act and the government wide regulations wasn't an expert, who was?

We were able to maintain our composure, but recall the incident as a quintessential example of how little engineers understand about the right of way process or the requirements that come with the use of federal funding.

Dick and I gave our five-minute presentation. To the horror of the engineers, the selection committee's questions were primarily about real estate. Our team was awarded the contract.

The story does not stop there. The manager of the Everglades Restoration Program was an attorney. In a meeting following ORC's selection, I explained that because federal funds were being used, it would be necessary to follow federal law and regulations as found in the Uniform Act and 49 CFR Part 24. This would mean that property had to be appraised by a qualified appraiser, and that property owners would be entitled to the full amount as appraised.

The attorney was surprised. Until this time, the SFWMD purchased land primarily under a state law known as Florida Forever, which limited payment to 90 percent of fair market value. However, since federal funding would be involved in the CERP, SFWMD would be required to pay the full appraised value for properties acquired for this project. The attorney challenged my advice and was convinced only when I pointed to the section of the law that states that the Uniform Act must be followed if federal funds are to be used in any part of the project.[18]

---

18 The reference is 49 CFR 24.2(a)(22). There are some additional references by FHWA/Lead Agency on its website to URA Q&As and other documents in support of this policy as well:

http://www.fhwa.dot.gov/real_estate/uniform_act/program_administration/ lpa_guide/ch02.cfm#whendoestheuniformactapply

Real Estate Acquisition Guide for Local Public Agencies
   When Does the Uniform Act Apply?
The Uniform Act applies when Federal dollars are utilized in any phase of a project. The Uniform Act applies even when Federal dollars are not used specifically for property acquisition or relocation activities, but are used elsewhere in the project, such as in planning, environmental assessments, or construction. The Uniform Act also applies to acquisitions by private as well as public entities when the acquisition is for a Federal or federally assisted project.

Chapter 7

● ● ●

HOW TECHNOLOGY AT ORC EVOLVED

I am a great believer that giving employees the latest technology and software enables them to be more productive. I consider the money we spend on technology to be a wise investment. We continually upgrade our hardware and software and offer our employees training on the new products.

My first job at ORC was as editor of the textbooks on negotiation, titles, appraisal and relocation that my father wrote for the training courses he developed. My undergraduate degree in English and Political Science was a natural fit for the job. However, it was the courses in computer science and accounting I took after graduation that prepared me to lead the company.

I graduated from West Virginia University in three years with an B.S. in English and Political Science and a minor in Music and wanted to further my studies. At the time, I lived in Bluefield, West Virginia and there were no graduate schools in the area. My children were young, so a long commute was out of the question. I decided to return to school to study computer science and accounting at Bluefield State College. Being 10 years older than the other students proved to be an advantage. My studies in computer science during this time made me one of the few adults of the Baby Boomer generation to become computer-savvy. A foundation in computer science gave me an appreciation for how the technology could be used to ORC's advantage. The accounting courses later proved to be essential to my success as our CEO.

THE DARK AGES

At this time, men relied on women in the workplace to do the typing. I remember people saying, "Don't let anyone know you can type, or you will always be a secretary." My father used to dictate his textbooks to a typist. Although he provided his typists with the best technology of the time—an IBM Display Writer—he never used the word processor himself.

In 1980, he bought an IBM System 21 computer for the South Charleston office to organize information and process checks for the Times Beach project. It was one of the very first business computers offered by IBM and it used 8-inch diskettes. By this time, I was a full time employee as the company's computer programmer.

In 1983, ORC purchased a computer for the Florida office. It was a Tandy TSH80, the most common computer used in the appraisal industry. Ed Wilson remembers it had a Daisy wheel printer that printed one page every 45 seconds. "We used it for years," he says.

Like many veterans of World War II, my father resisted buying products made in Japan. When the office acquired a Toshiba copier, he became visibly upset. A clever employee calmed him down by making a label with an American name to cover the logo.

DEVELOPMENT OF ORC'S IT SUPPORT (1980 - 1990)

As ORC grew, and the number of projects and employees fluctuated, keeping track of company finances became increasingly burdensome. I searched for appropriate software and determined that Deltek's accounting program would meet our needs. However, its $30,000 price tag and $10,000 annual maintenance fee was unaffordable at the time. My father said he would rather pay me to write a customized accounting program for us than to pay for the cost of the Deltek program. So I wrote an accounting program in RBase on a DOS platform. The program coded the detail of every check, listed debits and credits, printed the checks, converted numbers to words on the checks, calculated state and local taxes and printed W2s at the end of the year.

When it came time to prepare the year-end financial statements, I would send the data to an outside accounting firm. At the time, I worked in the South Charleston office two days a week and from home on the other days. The data had to be downloaded from the office to my home computer via a dialup phone modem—a painfully slow method of transmission.

The year-end file would take more than 12 hours to download. I would sleep that night with one eye open, in order to disconnect the line as soon as the download was complete to avoid incurring excess long-distance charges.

THE SEARCH FOR THE RIGHT ACCOUNTING SOFTWARE

When Microsoft introduced Windows 3.0 in 1990, it was time to switch to a Windows platform. I had no time to re-write the accounting program, so I began to look for an off-the-shelf accounting program designed for government contractors that we could afford.

I planned to hire a CFO and allow that person to assist in selecting the accounting program. Unfortunately, the first CFO had a manufacturing background and chose a program that was unable to handle the job-cost accounting needed for government work. ORC went through three CFOs before finding one who could understand the right of way business.

With the third CFO we bit the bullet and purchased the Deltek software. We wanted to avoid the cost, but it was clearly the best option. The new system allowed ORC to implement electronic time and expense sheets, which saved hours of employee time and improved accuracy.

In 2002, ORC upgraded to Deltek Advantage and, the following year, to Deltek Vision. The second system enabled ORC to manage an entire project, and gave employees access to information on every aspect of the project accounting from any computer at any time. We were using a trainer from Deltek, Carmen Johnson, who proved to be so important to our accounting department that we offered her a full time position. Carmen went on to become our Vice President of Finance and Administration.

"ORC integrated its financial, project and client relationship management in a centralized cohesive system which allows us to have real time data when making strategic decisions," says Carmen. "Our culture of continuous improvement focuses on implementing technologies that allow us to effectively manage our processes over multiple locations."

Today, ORC offices throughout the nation are linked by a centralized accounting system that provides accounting and billing services in accordance with government agency guidelines.

ORC PARCEL SUITE® AND ITS PREDECESSORS

In the 1980s I also created project management databases for our larger projects. The first project database was for the Times Beach project, and it enabled ORC to handle payments of more than $31 million in FEMA funds for 900 parcels. The system tracked daily draws from FEMA to the ORC account, so that checks could be written to owners when parcels closed. Without a computer, handling this volume of work would have been impossible.

After my father's death in 1989, I was too busy running the company to customize project databases. Instead, we partnered with contractors or subcontractors who had databases of their own, or simply used Excel spreadsheets.

Although teaming with other technology companies on some larger airport projects allowed ORC to offer database technology to clients, it wasn't a long-term solution. We lost bids, because our competitors were using software with interfaces to GIS mapping that impressed clients.

Sharing databases with partners did have one advantage in that it gave us a first-hand look at available products. We were not impressed. Most databases were designed for pipeline and other linear projects. We wanted more flexibility in our database, because each project had different needs.

What ORC required was a database that could handle the complex requirements of Uniform Act work and that could be modified for individual clients. It had to be cost effective and flexible. Since no commercially available product fit these requirements, it became clear that we would need to design our own project database.

Our IT Director, Christopher Castellano, led the effort to build a proprietary database that would meet our needs. The result was ORC Parcel

Suite, an application centered on customization to adapt to various types of projects. ORC Parcel Suite is affordable and can be easily modified to satisfy the requirements of each client.

"ORC has always been a challenging firm from a technology standpoint given its divided geographic nature and disparate project requirements. However, the vast amount of internal technical ROW knowledge possessed by employees allows IT to continually learn the industry and respond with solutions that simply work," says Mr. Castellano.

The next version of ORC Parcel Suite will be available in 2017. We expect it will be one of our competitive advantages in the market. It will utilize the latest languages and frameworks and include a dashboard that allows clients to view summary information on projects in real time. ORC now maintains an in-house programming team to make the custom modifications that our clients want.

Overall, our IT Department maintains multiple platforms that afford employees with ubiquitous, mobile access to various cloud-based resources for email, document management and collaboration. This network is a crucial component in effectively and efficiently operating a company that has offices in more than 20 states.

Chapter 8

· · ·

ORC'S VISION, MISSION AND VALUES

"**C**athy is fully committed to ORC being the industry leader," says Steve Cleary. "As a result, we have made our mark."

ORC'S VISION
Inspiring confidence in progress.

ORC'S MISSION

* We specialize in providing real estate services for infrastructure projects according to the highest professional standards.
* We work to minimize the stress caused by public works projects upon those who are required to sell their property or relocate for the benefit of the general public.
* We partner with consultants and vendors who share our values and our standards for quality.
* We strive to offer a satisfying and rewarding work experience for our employees.

ORC'S VALUES

ORC's values underlie everything we do. Our employees are expected to have *respect* for private property rights as guaranteed by the 5th and 14th Amendments to the Constitution of the United States; treat every property owner, employee and client with *respect* at all times; seek the *knowledge* needed to be prepared for every assignment; use *problem-solving* skills to meet every challenge; show *adaptability* to meeting the specific requirements of each agency we work with and adapting their negotiation skills as they work with different people; use *initiative* as they meet daily challenges; show *stewardship* when disbursing the client's money, ensuring also that full benefits are paid to those who qualify; and be aware of how we can be *socially responsible* as a company and as individuals.

We ask that our employees do all of this with *integrity* and awareness that we are part of a larger, *socially responsible* purpose, which is to build the infrastructure of our nation while respecting and protecting the private property rights of individuals who are impacted by a public infrastructure project.

When we do these things, we are ***inspiring confidence in progress***!

ORC's core values were long established in the company before they were put in writing. To help everyone remember the eight values, they have been separated into three groups. The three Core Values are Respect, Knowledge and Integrity. These naturally lead to Stewardship and Social Responsibility. Finally, the attributes that we look for in our employees are Initiative, Problem Solving and Adaptability.

CORE VALUES: RESPECT, KNOWLEDGE AND INTEGRITY

Respect

Underlying all that we do is our respect for property rights. The 5th Amendment to the Constitution states, "…nor shall private property be taken for public use, without just compensation." The Uniform Act and the implementing regulations found at 49 CRF Part 24 ensure that just compensation is provided according to due process in acquiring land needed for public use. It is our respect for the property rights of individuals that creates our emphasis on training our employees, so that these rights are preserved in the process of acquiring land for public infrastructure projects.

Respect for people is also a priority. "Mr. C.'s philosophy was that you treat everybody equally, whether they're the president of a bank or a Section 8 tenant. You were expected to treat everyone the way you would want to be treated," says Jill Knobbe.

We also encourage our employees to respect the environment and protect it for future generations.

Knowledge

Because ORC places a high value on knowledge, the company invests substantially in the education of employees, as well as others in the right of way industry.

ORC Training was created to develop training courses and conduct research studies. At the same time, ORC invested in a search engine for technical knowledge called the ORC Knowledge Base, which provides ORC employees with answers to questions related to right of way.

ORC Knowledge Base was conceived of by Mr. Colan's granddaughter, Karen Ammar, the current Chairman of ORC. Karen observed that employees were relying on experienced agents to answer technical questions. She felt it would be better use of the senior agents' time if common questions and answers were recorded and made available to all employees. A greater purpose of the ORC Knowledge Base is to preserve the expertise of our most experienced employees, long after they've retired.

The ORC Training staff writes questions and answers for inclusion in this proprietary database. Before any answer is entered in the database, it is reviewed by several technical experts, who add their perspectives on how the answer might differ for a highway, transit or airport client.

The technical experts in ORC Training have also written hundreds of articles that are contained in the ORC Knowledge Base. These articles are often featured as lead articles in our company newsletter, The Acquirer. In addition, the database contains the contents of courses developed by ORC for the National Highway Institute and those developed for internal training. Recently a section was added to include questions and answers related to Information Technology that we use at ORC.

ORC Training created courses for training ORC employees, providing the company with a complete catalogue of courses related to the implementation of the Uniform Act and land acquisition for public agencies. The Junior Agent training program for ORC Uniform Act Certification includes online training courses, as well as classroom courses. In 2014, ORC signed a licensing agreement with IRWA to provide these ORC Training courses on the IRWA online platform. The agreement also makes these courses eligible for certification credit through IRWA.

Our training program gives ORC employees the knowledge they need to negotiate with property owners and ensures that occupants receive all relocation benefits to which they are entitled. These courses illustrate our commitment to the advancement of knowledge within our industry, both nationwide and worldwide.

Integrity

Integrity results when behavior aligns with your values. My father believed that business should be conducted ethically.

I recall him saying that Governor Moore[19] sent one of his "associates" to visit him at the office one day to let him know how business was done. My father loved telling the story of how he "kicked the man to the street." It was said that Governor Moore had a drawer in his office, and consultants who wanted work with the state were expected to schedule a private visit with the governor and leave an envelope of cash in the drawer. Governor Moore was convicted in 1990 of corruption charges.

ORC has never used unethical business practices, and never will.

---

19 Arch A. Moore, Jr. was the Governor of West Virginia from 1969 to 1977 and again from 1985 to 1989. He pleaded guilty to five felony changes and in 1990 was sentenced to five years and ten months in prison.

FROM RESPECT, KNOWLEDGE AND INTEGRITY COME STEWARDSHIP AND SOCIAL RESPONSIBILITY
Stewardship

We are the stewards of what we are given in life. I was given a great responsibility when my father passed and the company was left to me. It is a responsibility that I cherish. I am grateful for the chance to work with wonderful people. My goal is to create an environment in which employees can reach their full potential.

Good stewardship is also about remaining aware that we are stewards of public funds. We strive continually to reduce program costs without reducing the benefits received by the owners and occupants impacted by the project.

The St. Louis office acted as good stewards of agency funds on the Lambert-St. Louis International Airport expansion project while making sure that owners received full benefits. During a time when interest rates were falling there were homeowners on the project with poor credit who could not obtain the market interest rate. ORC felt it was unreasonable to force a displaced homeowner to pay higher interest on a new property. They also felt it was not the client's responsibility to pay more due to a homeowner's financial shortcomings.

In order to be good stewards of the client's money while providing the full benefits to which homeowners were entitled, the staff contacted their old and new lenders and found out how long it would take to clear up their credit issues and refinance at the market rate. The agents computed the increased interest rate twice, once for the period of time it took to straighten out their credit at a higher rate, and again for the eligible time period after their credit issues would be resolved. Compensation checks reflected both interest rates. The FAA and the airport felt this was an equitable and creative solution favoring all parties.

WE VALUE THESE ATTRIBUTES IN OUR EMPLOYEES: INITIATIVE, PROBLEM SOLVING AND ADAPTABILITY.
Initiative

My father clearly defined ORC's value of Initiative in the August 1970 issue of *FC&E*, when he said, "Much of our technique consists of anticipating problems before they occur and solving them before they cause trouble."

The St. Louis office spent many years working on expansion and noise abatement projects at Lambert-St. Louis International Airport. The expansion program involved the construction of a tunnel under a runway. Digging the tunnel caused the road to shift, putting several apartment buildings in danger of sliding off their foundations.

To provide safety for the tenants and maintain the construction schedule, the St. Louis staff created an incentive for the tenants to move out of the affected apartments earlier than scheduled. In addition to typical relocation benefits, they would receive an additional $1,000 or $2,000, depending on how quickly they vacated. This initiative by ORC allowed the airport to get people moved before their foundations were impacted by construction. The plan also saved the client hundreds of thousands of dollars, because it allowed them to remain on target with the construction project.

Problem Solving

Over the years, ORC teams developed some creative approaches to solving problems faced by property owners and clients.

In the Times Beach project, the urgent need to get residents out of temporary housing and into permanent homes required title work and appraisals to be expedited. Obtaining titles was a challenge, since many of the property owners had received a free lot in exchange for purchasing a newspaper subscription. These lots were later swapped with other lots without being recorded.

To expedite title work, ORC employees devised an incentive program that paid the title companies extra for completing their searches in three weeks or less and providing assistance in clearing titles.

The second obstacle was the lack of available appraisers with expertise in the Uniform Act and experience in condemnation. To resolve this problem, ORC's review appraiser, Bob Pratt, mentored all newer appraisers. This accelerated the appraisal process.

"These are just a few examples of how we have solved complex problems in a manner that benefited the client and those impacted by the project," says Jill Knobbe.

Adaptability

Adaptability to change is another reason our clients continue to use ORC's services and recommend ORC to others.

The economic reality of being low-income is that it does not take much change to cause chaos. We saw this on a large sewer reconstruction project which impacted several low income areas. Shortly after the 2008 recession, many of these properties were effectively "under-water", i.e. the loan balances exceeded their value. While the properties could be condemned to clear title, the displaced owner-occupants' credit ratings would be destroyed and they would not be able to obtain financing for a replacement home.

Expanding to a non-federal agency the logic of a waiver authorized by the Federal Highway Administration, ORC used a "negative equity" administrative settlement to fully compensate the lender, thus preserving the credit ratings of the displaced owners. ORC also utilized the replacement housing purchase differential (Uniform Act Replacement Housing) as down-payment to assist the owners in purchasing a replacement dwelling. The program was a huge success and solved a major obstacle for our client.

Social Responsibility

We believe the work we do is socially responsible. We are helping to build the infrastructure of our country and working with the public on a daily basis.

"ORC is known as a great place to work, because it's not just about making money; it's about making a difference. We care about the people we work for, work with, and the community. When you put people first, the rest takes care of itself," says Steve Cleary.

On September 21, 2006, Virginia S. Young Elementary School, a Montessori Charter School in Fort Lauderdale, celebrated International Peace Day with the dedication of a Peace Garden sponsored by O. R. Colan Associates. O. R. Colan Associates and Virginia Shuman Young Elementary Montessori Magnet School (VSY) were awarded the 2006–2007 National School and Business Partnerships Award by the Council for Corporate &

School Partnerships by the Coca Cola Company for the creation of the Peace Garden.

Karen Ammar delivered the dedication speech, in which she quoted Dr. Maria Montessori's address to the League of Nations in Geneva in 1932: "The Science of Peace, were it to become a special discipline, would be the most noble of all, for the very life of humanity depends on it. So, also, perhaps does the question of whether our civilization evolves or disappears." The Peace Garden was intended to be a natural sanctuary in which the students, parents and teachers can search for meaningful ways to bring peace to each other, their communities and the world.

ORC supports local schools and other causes in many of its office locations. I have worked with Collins Elementary in Dania Beach, Florida, for more than 10 years. The first year, ORC donated equipment for a Science Center. The following year, the company provided funds to buy band instruments. In 2015, ORC sponsored a video showing how this small, disadvantaged school achieved notable academic success. For several years, ORC has sponsored the school's year-end Academic Awards Banquet. In honor of the work that ORC has done with Collins Elementary School, the school now gives an annual award at their Academic Banquet entitled the Catherine Muth Academic and Citizenship Award. ORC was awarded the Broward County "Partner of the Year" Award in 2006 and again in 2015 for our work with Collins Elementary School.

ORC also has a policy of providing matching donations from time to time when flooding or other natural disasters hit.

These are examples of how our company gives back to the communities in which we live and work.

Chapter 9

●　●　●

CATHY'S 4-3-2 PLAN FOR SUCCESS

This chapter is the text of a speech I prepared to deliver to a group of Executive MBA students at the Hyatt Regency in Fort Lauderdale, Florida, on April 14, 2006. When I arrived at the hotel, signs directed me to the event on the top floor. The topic of the evening was to be "Powerful Women CEOs and How They Are Shaping South Florida."

When I got off the elevator I was greeted with "Surprise!" The event was actually a surprise party to celebrate my 25 years with the company. My first question was "Do I still get to give my speech?" Of course, I did!

The text of that speech, which I call "My 4-3-2 Plan for Success," follows:

Our work impacts South Florida and many other locations all across the nation. O. R. Colan Associates is a real estate firm with a very special niche. We only work for public agencies,[20] and our services are valued because of our knowledge of the administrative laws and regulations that must be followed when federal funds are involved in any project.

We assist airports all over Florida[21] when they need to acquire real estate for noise mitigation or expansion programs, including past projects for Fort-Lauderdale-Hollywood International Airport and projects at Tampa and

---

20 This speech was prior to the establishment of ORC Utility & Infrastructure Land Services, LLC in 2010.

21 The speech was written to be given to an audience of students in Florida.

West Palm Beach. The Veteran's Expressway in Tampa and the Polk County Parkway, as well as improvements to I-275 in Tampa and I-95 in Jacksonville were built on land purchased by our company. We are also part of the team that is working on the Comprehensive Everglades Restoration Program, also known as the CERP.

Our vision in all that we do is to inspire confidence in progress by fairly treating those who must relocate for the good of the general public and by making sure they are given all the benefits they are entitled to under the guidelines for federally funded programs.

First, I want to say that I never think of myself as powerful—I think the word strong would be more appropriate. To lead a company of any size requires personal inner strength.

I am going to share with you some ideas I have on some key areas that could serve as a guide to anyone who wants to take on the responsibility of leading a company.

First, let's agree that a CEO is not a manager. A CEO is must be a leader and must be focused more on the future than on the present. If you are managing the day-to-day activities of a company, then you will not have time to think about the future.

Second, let's agree that people will follow a bad leader as well as a good leader. There are numerous current public leaders I could site as examples—and I will let you use your imaginations to fill in the names.

I want to share a personal experience. One day a few years ago I accidentally turned into the sixth lane of Broward Boulevard at the intersection of Broward and Federal Highway. At this intersection Broward has six lanes going east and only two lanes going west. I turned into the sixth lane, by mistake. Incredibly, five cars followed me, proving without a doubt that people will follow a bad leader! So a strong leader is not necessarily a good leader.

I am going to share with you 4 Qualities, 3 Abilities and 2 Principles that have been important to my success as a CEO. I call this my 4-3-2 Plan for Success. These are things that are not taught in any business degree program, but you can nurture them in yourself.

The **4 Qualities** are **Perseverance, Optimism, Intuition** and **Empathy.**

Perseverance is the difference between success and failure. Perseverance is more important than any other quality in a strong leader. I have always said that our biggest successes have often come five minutes after I was ready to give up. The key is not giving up.

Optimism is the second most important quality. Henry Ford said it best, when he said, "Whether you think you can or think you can't, you're right."

Intuition is the third quality. If you are an intuitive decision maker, it will be a plus. This has been very helpful for me, because a CEO must be able to make a decision based on limited information. A timely decision is more important than a perfect decision.

Empathy is the fourth quality. People skills are the most important skills you can have, because most issues you will have as a business owner or leader will be around people issues, not technical issues. A good leader will take responsibility when things go wrong and give credit to others when they go right.

We all find ourselves in frustrating situations or relationships with difficult people. You can change those experiences by controlling how you react. The only person you can change is yourself and, sometimes, that is enough to change how others interact with you.

The **3 Abilities** are the **ability to accept responsibility**, the **ability to accept risk** and the **ability to focus on the future**.

Ability to accept responsibility. Do you accept responsibility when things go wrong and give credit to others when things go right? Some managers want to take credit when things go right and blame others when things go wrong. This is a seriously limiting deficiency. Management and leadership are all about accepting responsibility for the actions of your team. If you can't give credit to your team when things go right and accept responsibility when things go wrong, then your ability to take on executive responsibility is limited.

Ability to accept risk. You must be a risk-taker if you want to be successful. As a business owner or executive, you have to be willing to take risks to pursue your vision.

I once said to someone that I am just not interested in gambling. I have always found casino gambling boring. As soon as I said this, I realized that being a business owner is the biggest gamble you can take, because every job you bid is a gamble and the stakes are high.

Ability to focus on the future. An executive must have the patience and vision to plan for projects that will not be completed for many years.

Your ability to be promoted to high-level positions in your career will depend upon your time span. How long into the future is your timeline for work? Are you more comfortable with a job that is repetitive every 30 days? Are you comfortable with a project that has a completion date two years from now? Are you comfortable managing a project with a 5 or 10-year schedule? A CEO must be able to have the vision, patience and perseverance to plan for projects that will not be completed for many years.

If you are a parent, then you know that you invest much of your creative energy into a project (your child) where you may not see the results of your efforts for two decades or more. Don't underestimate the value this experience can bring to your executive career.

Finally, there are **2 Guiding Principles**.

Never make a decision based on fear. If you use the word "fear" to justify any action or refusal to act, then you should rethink your decision. For example, "I'm afraid my team won't go along with this new idea," is not a good reason not to proceed. If you hear yourself using the word "fear" in your justification of any action, then back up and rethink it. Most people never accomplish even a fraction of what they are capable of, because they are afraid of failure, of the cost, of what people may say, of change - or because they are afraid of success.

Avoid negative energy. If you indulge in negative energy, you will not have enough energy to be a leader.

This last point has been one of the more important realizations in the development of my career. Yet, the ability to refuse to participate in negative energy was learned in daily experiences. Do you fume when you have to wait in traffic or in a line at the grocery store? If so, then you are allowing negative energy to drain you of your energy resources. If you are going to be a strong leader, then you will need all of the energy you can find. You can make a rational decision to not allow negative energy to drain you. Try it the next time you are caught in traffic or have to wait in a long line at the grocery store. You will find lots of opportunities to work on this quality!

As candidates in the Executive MBA program, you are learning skills that you can use in your career. You will need these skills, but in order to be a strong leader, you will need to consciously work on your own set of qualities—which may include some of those that I have listed as important to my success. Don't undervalue your personal qualities, which—like mine—were probably learned outside of school and the work place.

I want to warn you that changes in the business world are moving so fast that any formal education program will never be able to prepare you completely for what you need to be a leader today. Your degree will be an indicator of your ability to learn, and you must continue to learn every day. If you ever have the opportunity to become a member of TEC (now Vistage), I would strongly recommend this to any business leader. I have participated monthly in a TEC group since 1995, and this has been my single greatest source of continuing education as a CEO.

I am honored to be asked to speak to you tonight and I hope that my comments will be useful to you as you strive to become the business leaders of the future.

P. S. Those attending my 25th Anniversary party listened patiently to my prepared "4-3-2 Plan for Success" and said it was a good speech. Then we had a really great party!

PART III
THE FUTURE
OUR 2020 VISION

Chapter 10

● ● ●

ORC'S 2020 VISION

In October 2015, ORC announced its 5-year strategic plan for 2016-2020: ORC's 2020 Vision. The plan is to double the company's net revenue by 2020 through the addition of new service lines and the creation of a "doer-seller" culture, in which every employee understands the range of services offered by ORC and knows how to contribute to building market share for ORC. Our goal is to ensure that each office has a steady backlog of work, so that teams can remain in place for the long term. We believe this is essentially what every employee wants—job security without needing to move after a project is completed.

The "doer-seller" culture concept soon became the "ORC Ambassadors Program."

The organizational chart below shows the core concept behind ORC's new plan. The strategic plan is based on a regional concept, with all lines of service offered in each region.

Each region is led by a Regional Vice President, who is responsible for spearheading efforts to build all service lines offered by ORC in that region. In addition to right of way services for public agencies offered by O. R. Colan Associates, LLC, these include right of way services for the utility sector offered by ORC Utility & Infrastructure

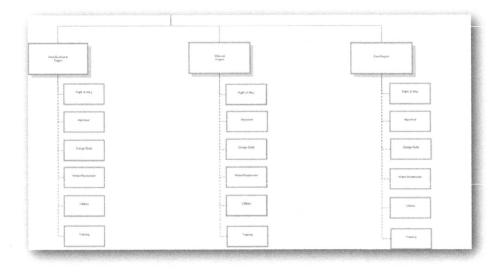

Land Services, LLC, training offered by ORC Training and appraisals offered by ORC Appraisals.

As part of this reorganization, we simplified our company's structure by rolling all subsidiaries into O. R. Colan Group, LLC, and renaming it O. R. Colan Associates, LLC.[22]

The ORC Ambassadors Program gives employees responsibility for business development for their region. This provides new opportunities for those who wish to advance in their careers, while remaining in the ORC family of businesses.

ORC's 2020 Vision creates a structure and culture that increases the opportunity for all employees to grow and advance their careers with ORC. When our employees succeed, our company is also successful. Our 2020 Vision inspires confidence in the future of ORC as we move into a new era of growth.

---

22 Prior to this reorganization, the subsidiaries of O. R. Colan Group, LLC were O. R. Colan Associates of Florida, LLC; O. R. Colan Associates of Illinois, LLC; O. R. Colan Associates of California, LLC and O. R. Colan Corporate, LLC. ORC Training, LLC was an affiliate company that was also rolled into O. R. Colan Associates, LLC.

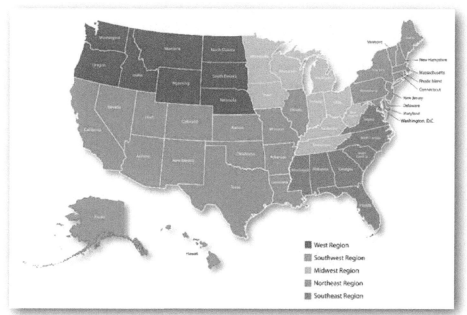

ORC's Regional Map for 2016

CONCLUSION

The right of way industry is an invisible real estate niche. Everyone knows that engineers design highways and that construction companies build highways. No one thinks about how the land is purchased so that the highway can be constructed. That's what we do. And we do it with respect for property rights, respect for all people, knowledge of the state and federal laws that govern the process, and always with integrity.

We know the work we do at ORC is important. A modern, well-maintained infrastructure is critical to our country's economic well-being and safety. We work with people who are being asked to move or sell their property so that a highway, airport, school, transmission line or other project can be constructed for the benefit of the general public. Sometimes, we work with people who are being permanently relocated so that they will no longer be vulnerable to floods, or temporarily relocated so that their homes can be elevated before the next storm.

We hope that we are changing the world for the better. While we are doing this external work, internally we are working to create a company environment where every employee can reach his or her full potential.

In these ways, we are ***inspiring confidence in progress***.